WITHDRAWN

Bloom's

GUIDES

J.R.R. Tolkien's
The Hobbit

The Adventures of Huckleberry Finn

The Adventures of Tom Sawyer

All Quiet on the Western Front

Animal Farm

The Autobiography of Malcolm X

The Awakening

The Bell Jar

Beloved

Beowulf

Black Boy

The Bluest Eye

Brave New World

The Canterbury Tales

Catch-22

The Catcher in the Rye

The Chosen

A Christmas Carol

The Crucible

Cry, the Beloved Country

Death of a Salesman

Fahrenheit 451

A Farewell to Arms

Frankenstein

The Glass Menagerie

The Grapes of Wrath

Great Expectations

The Great Gatsby

The Handmaid's Tale

Heart of Darkness

The Hobbit

The House on Mango Street

I Know Why the Caged Bird Sings

The Iliad

Invisible Man

Jane Eyre

The Joy Luck Club

The Kite Runner

Lord of the Flies

Macbeth

Maggie: A Girl of the Streets

The Metamorphosis

Native Son

Night

1984

The Odyssey

Oedipus Rex

Of Mice and Men

One Hundred Years of Solitude

Pride and Prejudice

Ragtime

A Raisin in the Sun

The Red Badge of Courage

The Road

Romeo and Juliet

The Scarlet Letter

A Separate Peace

Slaughterhouse-Five

The Stranger

A Streetcar Named Desire

The Sun Also Rises

A Tale of Two Cities

Their Eyes Were Watching God

To Kill a Mockingbird

Uncle Tom's Cabin

The Waste Land

Wuthering Heights

Bloom's
GUIDES

J.R.R. Tolkien's
The Hobbit

Edited & with an Introduction
by Harold Bloom

BLOOM'S
LITERARY CRITICISM
An Infobase Learning Company

Bloom's Literary Criticism
An imprint of Infobase Learning
132 West 31st Street
New York, NY 10001

Library of Congress Cataloging-in-Publication Data
J.R.R. Tolkien's The hobbit / edited and with an introduction by Harold Bloom.
    p. cm. — (Bloom's guides)
    Includes bibliographical references and index.
    ISBN 978-1-61753-003-6 (hardcover)
    1. Tolkien, J. R. R. (John Ronald Reuel), 1892–1973. Hobbit.
    2. Middle Earth (Imaginary place) I. Bloom, Harold. II. Title: Tolkien's The hobbit. III. Title: Hobbit.
    PR6039.O32H6333 2011
    823'.912—dc22

                            2011017010

Bloom's Literary Criticism books are available at special discounts when purchased in bulk quantities for businesses, associations, institutions, or sales promotions. Please call our Special Sales Department in New York at (212) 967–8800 or (800) 322–8755.

You can find Bloom's Literary Criticism on the World Wide Web at http://www.infobaselearning.com

Contributing editor: Portia Williams Weiskel
Cover designed by Takeshi Takahashi
Composition by IBT Global, Troy NY
Cover printed by Yurchak Printing, Landisville PA
Book printed and bound by Yurchak Printing, Landisville PA
Date printed: September 2011
Printed in the United States of America

This book is printed on acid-free paper.

All links and Web addresses were checked and verified to be correct at the time of publication. Because of the dynamic nature of the Web, some addresses and links may have changed since publication and may no longer be valid.

Contents

Introduction

HAROLD BLOOM

I continue to prefer *The Hobbit* to *The Lord of the Rings* but acknowledge that I represent only a minority of current readers. Tolkien's epic fantasy is moralistic, and its neobiblical style is pretentious and inflated. Perhaps because it began as a fairy tale for children, *The Hobbit* is rather more refreshing.

Whether even *The Hobbit* is other than a period piece is questionable. Read it side by side with John Crowley's *Little, Big* and you will find *The Hobbit* vanishing away! The same fate attends Tolkien's epic when juxtaposed with Philip Pullman's *His Dark Materials*. My own canonical prophecy, founded on a long lifetime of literary study, has to be melancholy. Like his imitator, the Harry Potter saga, Tolkien will not be read a generation or two hence.

Attempt to reread Rider Haggard's *She* or *King Solomon's Mines*. Like Tolkien's books, they are more vivid as movies and fade on the page. Haggard is Tolkien's authentic precursor; his Allan Quartermain is a palpable model for Bilbo Baggins.

Contributors to this guide do damage to *The Hobbit* when they invoke Lewis Carroll's *Alice* books or Kenneth Grahame's *The Wind in the Willows*. Comparisons to Robert Louis Stevenson's *Kidnapped* and *Treasure Island* are equally destructive to Tolkien.

For more than a half century, I have been chided as provocative and controversial merely because I go on insisting that, without aesthetic and cognitive standards, imaginative literature will perish, and something in us also will wane.

Thinking depends on memory. Fashion passes, and the libraries are replete with forgotten bestsellers. The function of criticism, particularly in the digital age, is to teach us to prefer more difficult pleasures than those so easy that they weaken our minds.

Biographical Sketch

John Ronald Reuel Tolkien was born on January 3, 1892, to Arthur and Mabel Tolkien, in Bloemfontein, South Africa. Although his parents were British citizens, Tolkien's father had moved to South Africa to work in banking because the diamonds, gold, and other precious metals that were being mined in the Dutch colony were creating a boom economy. Two years later, Tolkien's younger brother, Hilary, was born. Tolkien's childhood was generally unhappy, his father dying in 1896 and his mother returning to England. The family moved continually between the working-class villages around Birmingham, until his mother died in 1904. The boys were then shuffled around between various relatives, until Tolkien settled in at King Edward's School, with custody given to Father Francis Morgan.

At King Edward's, Tolkien discovered his passion for languages, especially languages regarded as "dead." He also discovered *Beowulf* and the field of philology, both of which remained lifelong loves. In 1910, he entered Exeter College, Oxford, where he deepened his studies of language and premodern texts. He also formed two of the social bonds he would maintain throughout his life. First, he fell in love with Edith Bratt, who, after a long and difficult courtship, he would marry in 1916. Second, he found himself at home in the active club and society life at college, so much so that he and a circle of literary- and language-minded colleagues formed their own club, the Tea Club Bavarian Society, which was dedicated to a mythical, if not romantic, manner of relating to the world. Even after most of the members of the TCBS were killed in World War I, Tolkien retained the beliefs upheld by the TCBS, and he continued to feel the need for membership in social clubs and circles throughout his life, eventually forming several groups of his own, including the famous Inklings, which included C.S. Lewis.

In 1915, Tolkien, like much of his generation, joined the military to fight for England and the Allies against Germany and Turkey in World War I. He fought at the Battle of the

Somme as a signaling officer. While there he contracted trench fever, a disease transmitted by lice, and was eventually sent to recover in a hospital in England. During this time, Tolkien began for the first time earnestly working at creating the mythology of Middle-earth, as he began crafting the languages of Middle-earth and writing the earliest forms of the stories that would make up *The Silmarillion*.

After the war ended in 1918, Tolkien spent time working on the New English Dictionary and teaching. He eventually secured a professorship at Leeds College. While there, he helped produce a new edition of *Sir Gawain and the Green Knight*, which enabled him to land the job he retained for the rest of his professional career, professor of Anglo-Saxon at Oxford. While at Oxford, he formed a lifelong friendship with the writer C.S. Lewis and began working on *The Hobbit*, at first as a tale for his own children; it was eventually published in 1937. (See "The Story Behind the Story," p. 11).

The Hobbit proved to be a bestseller, and under pressure to produce a sequel to it, Tolkien began writing again. His attempt to write a sequel to *The Hobbit* turned into *The Lord of the Rings*, which was eventually published in 1954–55. The trilogy became one of the bestselling book series in history and launched a worldwide following. In 1972, his wife, Edith, died, and two years later, on September 2, 1973, Tolkien died at the age of 81. Tolkien's youngest son, Christopher, has continued to edit and publish Tolkien's many manuscripts and notes, including *The Silmarillion* and *The Book of Lost Tales*.

The Story Behind the Story

Coincidentally, the story of the origin of *The Hobbit* seems itself like a fairy tale. One summer night in 1928, as Tolkien was grading a mountain of school certificate exam papers, a dull and mentally wearying task, he found himself staring at an exam booklet, daydreaming. As Tolkien recalled, "One of the candidates had mercifully left one of the pages with no writing on it, (which is the best thing that can possibly happen to an examiner), and I wrote on it: In a hole in the ground there lived a hobbit. Names always generate a story in my mind. Eventually I thought I'd better find out what hobbits were like. But that's only the beginning" (Carpenter 175).

Reflecting back, Tolkien never identified one source for the name he eventually settled on, Bilbo Baggins, although he did see parallels between his character and Sinclair Lewis's *Babbit*. But he also saw a lot of himself in his creation: "I am in fact a Hobbit, in all but size. I like gardens, trees, and unmechanized farmlands; I smoke a pipe and like good plain food" (Carpenter 179). The name for Bilbo's hole, Bag End, Tolkien took from the nickname for his aunt's farm. Likewise, Tolkien sensed a similarity to English country folk in his creation, remarking: "The Hobbits are just rustic English people, made small in size because it reflects the generally small reach of their imagination, not the small reach of their courage or latent power" (Carpenter 180).

Some Tolkien scholars suggest that Gandalf's image, if not his name, came from a postcard of a bearded man in a broad brimmed hat standing in front of the Alps (Carpenter 51). Tolkien began by giving one of the dwarves the name Gandalf and the wizard character the name Bladorthin, but he thought Gandalf sounded more like the name of a magical being, so he changed it. Other interesting name evolutions include Medwed the Werebear being altered to Beorn and Pryftan the dragon becoming Smaug the dragon.

The narrative was worked on intermittently over the years 1930–36. At first, Tolkien did not conceive of the story as anything other than a way to entertain his children, and he read them chapters and scenes from handwritten notes. While the tale continued to grow, it remained a diversion solely intended for his children. The manuscript did not have an ending when the first readers other than his children became involved in the project. Tolkien had developed a friendship with author C.S. Lewis at meetings of a literary club called the Coalbitters. The Coalbitters studied Old Icelandic literature, always a favorite of Tolkien's. Their friendship grew stronger, and they formed another literary club in 1933 called the Inklings. The Inklings met twice a week, one night for social discourse and the second for reading and commenting on members' creative and academic writing. At the urging of C.S Lewis and other members of the Inklings, Tolkien typed and polished his manuscript. Likewise, poet W.H. Auden was one of Tolkien's students at Oxford and was an enthusiastic supporter of *The Hobbit*.

Eventually, the manuscript fell into the hands of Elaine Griffiths, a former student of Tolkien's, who was working at the publishing house of Allen and Unwin. Griffiths and another firm employee, Susan Dagnall, read the manuscript and urged Tolkien to finish it and revise it for submission, which he diligently completed. The manuscript was then submitted to Stanley Unwin. Since *The Hobbit* was conceived as a children's tale, Unwin gave it to his ten-year-old son to read. His son thoroughly enjoyed the book, and it was accepted for publication. *The Hobbit* was published on September 21, 1937; the text included several of Tolkien's own illustrations. It was well received, both critically and by readers, and the first edition sold out. Critics hailed *The Hobbit* as a new classic of children's literature.

In 1951, Tolkien revised *The Hobbit* to bring the book into better alignment with his mythology as he was developing Middle-earth in his manuscripts and notes for *The Lord of the Rings*. He increased the importance of the necromancer character and made the most substantial changes to the chapter "Riddles in the Dark." In the original version, Gollum is not as twisted a figure, and the riddle game ends with Gollum offering to give the ring to Bilbo and lead him out of the cave. However, when Tolkien decided that the ring was the One True Ring, he altered the story to the version that exists today.

List of Characters

Bilbo Baggins, a good-natured hobbit, is the main protagonist of the novel. He prizes home and hearth and, like all hobbits, loves food and drink. He is hired as the burglar for the adventure and fulfills his tasks with a mix of courage, luck, and practical advice. Bilbo's finding of the ring of invisibility under the Misty Mountains serves as the principal point of departure for the narrative of *The Lord of the Rings*, in which he is also an important character.

Gandalf is a wizard and also a central character in *The Lord of the Rings*. While Gandalf is not depicted as powerfully as he is in *LOTR*, he is still perhaps the strongest character in *The Hobbit*. He is witty and wise, is a master of pyrotechnics and smoke rings, and is generally capable of getting the group out of trouble, either through his counsel or his wizardry.

The Dwarves

For the most part, the dwarves in Thorin's party are minor characters in the story, and several do not have any dialogue at all. Those dwarves that play a more significant role in the story are discussed here. General dwarven characteristics, such as stubbornness, a ravenous appetite for food and drink, and a love of gold, can be attributed to each of these members of Thorin's retinue.

Thorin Oakenshield is next in line to be named King under the Mountain. Thorin is a proud, valiant dwarf of noble blood. Generally good-natured if longwinded, he is still prone to the treasure lust that can overcome a dwarf and make him mistreat his friends. Thorin is particularly taken by the Arkenstone.

Balin, over the course of the journey, develops a deep respect and friendship for Bilbo.

Bombur is most notable for being the fattest of the dwarves, and his weight is used to generate humorous situations in the text. He also tends to have the worst luck of all the dwarves, as he tends to fall victim to the dangers of the journey more than any other character. Bombur, for example, falls into the river in Mirkwood that has been enchanted to cause anyone who drinks from or swims in it to fall into a deep, forgetful sleep.

Select "Good" Characters

Master of Rivendale and one of the great leaders of the elves, **Elrond** is one of the wisest characters in Middle-earth and through his advice is a constant force for good. He plays a major role in *The Lord of the Rings*. Elrond, although an immortal elf, has human blood and generally cares about all the peoples of Middle-earth.

A stern but just leader, the **wood elf king** rules over the wood elves of Mirkwood.

Described as having a grim voice, **Bard** is a natural warrior who worries that the return of the dwarves will mean a return of the dragon. He proves to be a warrior of great courage and fortitude, as he remains at his post in Lake-town when the dragon attacks. He kills Smaug and is eventually declared leader of the lake men.

Described as "very strong and he is a skin changer," **Beorn** can transform from a human into a bear. He has a great hatred for goblins and is generally neutral toward the other people of Middle-earth. He cares a great deal for the land and for animals, however, and acts as a guardian over the natural world around his log cabin. He aids the party before they cross Mirkwood and later proves to be of assistance at the Battle of Five Armies.

Dain of the Iron Hills is Thorin's cousin and leader of the dwarves of the Iron Hills.

The Lord of the Eagles had "eyes that could look at the sun unblinking and could see a rabbit moving on the ground a mile below"(114). The eagles rule the skies of Middle-earth, and from time to time they intervene on behalf of good characters, rescuing them or attacking their enemies. In *The Hobbit*, the Lord of the Eagles develops a deep friendship with Gandalf and remains his ally throughout *The Lord of the Rings*.

The Thrush are an ancient and noble race of birds that lived in harmony with the dwarves and the men of the Lonely Mountain and surrounding area before the arrival of the dragon. A thrush plays a very important role in the story, helping Bilbo find a secret door and helping Bard aim for the dragon's one weak spot. Thrushes can speak with men and dwarves.

The Ravens are, like the thrushes, an old race of birds allied with the dwarves and men of the area around the Lonely Mountain. They can communicate with men and dwarves.

Select "Evil" Characters

Smaug is the great dragon or *wyrm*. Many years before the action related in *The Hobbit* begins, Smaug attacked the Lonely Mountain and surrounding areas, killing all the men and dwarves who lived there. He captured the Lonely Mountain and all its vast treasures and turned the mountain into his lair. He sleeps on a giant pile of treasure. A vastly powerful and dangerous monster, he has but one weakness: an unarmored spot on his belly.

Gollum lives far beneath the Misty Mountains. He once owned the ring Bilbo finds, calling it his precious. Gollum is a treacherous, evil-minded creature whose main preoccupation is sneaking up on people (and goblins) and eating them. Gollum plans to eat Bilbo after they play the riddle game. The text hints at Gollum's history, which will be fully detailed in *The Lord of the Rings*.

Sometimes called orcs, **goblins** are an evil race of monsters that inhabit all the dark and dangerous locations in

Middle-earth. They are first encountered in *The Hobbit* in the tunnels and caves of the Misty Mountains. By riding wargs, they are able to roam the countryside, killing and marauding wherever they go. An army of goblins takes part in the Battle of Five Armies, and goblins figure prominently in *The Lord of the Rings*.

Evil, wolflike creatures, large and bloodthirsty, **wargs** align themselves with goblins in order to more efficiently terrorize the people of Middle-Earth.

Tom, **William**, and **Bill** are trolls, huge, ugly monsters with evil dispositions and a taste for humans, dwarves, and hobbits. Extremely strong and extremely unintelligent, trolls cannot come out during the day, as sunlight turns them to stone.

In *The Hobbit*, **spiders** live in Mirkwood, preying on victims who lose their way in the forest. These spiders are very large (bigger than Bilbo), can speak, and have an evil disposition. They particularly hate to be called names.

The Necromancer is a character who remains offstage and in the background of *The Hobbit* yet is reported to be a source of much of the evil in the story. He seems to be as powerful as Elrond or Gandalf, and Gandalf disappears from the story temporarily to attempt to thwart the Necromancer. The Necromancer will play a far larger role in *The Lord of the Rings*.

Head merchant and leader of the men of Lake-town when the dwarves arrive there, **the Master of Dale** is not evil in the goblin sense, but he is a base character. He is selfish, sneaky, and double faced and thinks only of his own power and wealth.

Summary and Analysis

Chapter One: An Unexpected Party

The opening lines of *The Hobbit* are well known both for establishing the fantasy world where the narrative will take place and for introducing the reader to one of the principal inhabitants of that world, hobbits: "In a hole in the ground there lived a hobbit. Not a nasty, dirty wet hole, filled with the ends of worms and an oozy smell, nor yet a dry, bare sandy hole with nothing in it to sit down on or to eat: it was a hobbit-hole, and that means comfort." (3) Works of fantasy need to establish that the story takes place in a setting different from the world of everyday reality, where things can be quite different from they are in normal reality. Tolkien does this by introducing the world of hobbits and hobbit holes. He clearly shows that these hobbit holes are not like the holes some creatures inhabit in reality; rather, they are special, almost magical holes, in which special, almost magical creatures live. As Tolkien continues to describe the comfortable, cozy, hobbit hole, the reader also learns about hobbits, most notably that they especially enjoy eating. Hobbits "are little people, about half our height, and smaller than the bearded dwarves." (4) Note that Tolkien has introduced other facts about this fantasy world: It is inhabited by hobbits and people but also by other creatures such as dwarfs. Tolkien then notes that this particular hole belongs to the main protagonist of the narrative, Bilbo Baggins, and he proceeds to describe Bilbo's genealogy. In doing so, the author also fills in further background on hobbits and the setting of the story. Unfortunately for Bilbo, his quiet, comfortable life in his warm, well-stocked hobbit hole is about to change, as one morning, Gandalf the wizard appears at his front door.

The scene already introduces one of the major themes of *The Hobbit*, the importance of change, or of the necessity of leaving the security of home in order to experience the world on an adventure or journey. The importance of this theme can be noted in the subtitle of the book, *The Hobbit, or There and Back Again*. This theme is revisited repeatedly in the story. When reading *The Hobbit*, note the development of the various characters in response to the changing environment and challenges of the story.

The initial humorous interchange between Gandalf and Bilbo establishes that Bilbo has never really left his immediate environs and knows little of the world beyond the Hill where he lives. Gandalf is about to change that fact, as Bilbo invites the visitor to tea. Little does Bilbo know that Gandalf is going to invite a party of 13 dwarves to the party as well, with the intention of having Bilbo join them on an adventure. The scene reveals Gandalf as a master of psychology, as he knows that Bilbo would never consciously decide to undertake such an adventure, no matter how tempted he might be, in part. Gandalf tricks Bilbo into going along, simply by telling the dwarves that Bilbo is going and by never giving Bilbo the opportunity to say no.

After a large meal, Gandalf and the assembled dwarves inform Bilbo of their plans. One of the dwarves, Thorin Oakenshield, is in fact a dwarf prince. His grandfather, Thror, was the last King under the Mountain and ruled a noble kingdom filled with jewels, gold, and other wondrous treasures. Unfortunately, the legendary wealth of Thror was his kingdom's undoing, as Thorin informs, "undoubtedly that was what brought the dragon. Dragons steal gold and jewels, you know, from men and elves and dwarves where ever they can find them; and they guard their plunder as long as they live (which is practically forever, unless they are killed)." (27) Smaug the dragon destroyed the kingdom, killing many dwarves and men, and took Lonely Mountain as his lair. Thorin's plan, with the help of a map procured by Gandalf, is for the party of 13 dwarves and one hobbit to journey to the Lonely Mountain to take revenge on Smaug the dragon.

Chapter Two: Roast Mutton

Bilbo and the dwarves begin their journey, traveling through what, to Bilbo at least, are wild and unknown lands. After several weeks of travel, with Bilbo noticing how infrequent meals and snacks are on an adventure, the party makes camp in a wooded area. While setting up camp, the dwarves notice another fire farther in the woods and send Bilbo to investigate. Bilbo sneaks up to the second campfire only to discover a group of trolls gathered there. The encounter with the trolls is the first dangerous obstacle of the journey and the first time the reader gets to see Bilbo in action.

At first it seems as if Bilbo's inexperience and comfort-loving ways are no match for the rigors and dangers of an adventure. He attempts to pick one of the troll's pockets, only to be easily caught. The dwarves come along to see what happened to Bilbo and fall into the trolls' trap. The trolls put all the dwarves in sacks and begin debating among themselves how best to eat them. This event marks the first time Gandalf will save the party from trouble. While the trolls are debating one another, Gandalf sneaks up and begins imitating the voice of each troll, which causes them to start bickering. The trolls, as a result of Gandalf's instigating, become so consumed in arguing with one another that they forget about the approach of dawn. As the sun emerges, Gandalf steps forward, and the trolls are turned to stone.

As the party collects itself, Bilbo finds a key that leads the party to the trolls' treasure. The treasure, which pales in comparison to the dragon's treasure, is still notable as three magic, elvish swords are found: Sting by Bilbo, Glamdring by Gandalf, and Orcrist by Thorin. These magic blades go on to play an important role in *The Hobbit* and make notable contributions in *The Lord of the Rings*. Additionally, the encounter with the trolls serves as a model for much of the action of the rest of the story, as the dwarves continually get themselves into trouble that either Bilbo or Gandalf must rescue them from.

Chapter Three: A Short Rest

Chapter three details the group's visit to Rivendale, home of elf-lord Elrond, and is most notable for introducing the reader to the culture of the nature-loving elves. Elves are immortal, generally good-natured denizens of Middle-earth who enjoy joking and singing but are powerful and formidable foes when roused to anger. Bilbo falls in love with elvish culture: "tired as he was, Bilbo would have liked to stay awhile. Elvish singing is not a thing to miss, in June, under the stars. . . . Elves know a lot and are wondrous folk for news, and know what is going on among the people of the land, as quick as water flows, or quicker."(56) The elves seem deeply connected to nature and to their environment.

When Elrond meets with the group, he is able to give them important information about their quest. He identifies the swords they found as "old swords, very old swords of the high elves of the west . . . they were made in Gondolin for the Goblin-wars." (58) This information will prove crucial in the next chapter. Elrond is also able to find and read hidden runes on the dwarves' map that identify how to locate a secret door leading to Smaug's lair. It is important to note that, although Elrond does not play a large role in the action of the story, the quest would never have been completed without his advice. This prefigures the role that Elrond plays in most of Tolkien's writing and how he influences most of the events that take place in Middle-Earth.

Chapter Four: Over Hill and Under Hill

The party begins the long and treacherous crossing of the Misty Mountains. After encountering a particularly heavy thunderstorm, which includes giants throwing boulders along the mountain range, the party takes shelter in a cave. However, the cave is a trap set by the goblins who live under the Misty Mountains. While Bilbo and the dwarves are captured by the goblins, Gandalf is able to escape due to Bilbo's warning. The dwarves and Bilbo are taken before the Great Goblin, who finds the Elvish swords and flies into a rage. The goblins are about to kill the adventurers when Gandalf returns. To this point in the narrative so far, Gandalf's value has been depicted through his intelligence and good humor, but the following scene reveals the power of Gandalf the wizard:

Murderers and elf-friends! the Great Goblin shouted. . . .
He was in such a rage that he jumped off his seat and himself rushed at Thorin with his mouth open.

Just at that moment all the lights in the cavern went out ... into a tower of blue glowing smoke, right up to the roof, that scattered piercing white sparks all among the goblins.

The yells and yammering ... that followed were beyond description. ... The sparks were burning holes in the goblins, and the smoke that now fell from the roof made the air too thick for even their eyes to see through. Soon they were falling over one another in heaps on the floor. ... Suddenly a sword flashed in its own light. Bilbo saw it go right through the Great Goblin as he stood dumbfounded in the middle of his rage. He fell dead and the goblin soldiers fled before the sword shrieking in the darkness. (72)

Note the contrasting way Gandalf is depicted in this passage as compared to how he is portrayed in the various noncombative situations in which he finds himself. The description and role of the magic sword Glamdring is also an important inclusion. Material items, such as swords and armor, play central roles in Tolkien's fiction. Swords are symbolic of might and valor, but they also serve as emblems of the highest arts of the cultures that produced them. Tolkien's material items are also a means of conveying a sense of the history of Middle-Earth, as they often trace their power and importance back to a great leader of battle in the history of one of the region's races. A majority of the characters of the story are familiar with the history and reputation of material items such as these highly prized, magic swords.

After Gandalf kills the Great Goblin, he leads the party on its escape from the goblin dungeons. As the group is running through the dark passages, however, they lose Bilbo, who hits his head on a wall and tumbles down a dark tunnel. Yet what at first seems like a stroke of bad luck for Bilbo turns out to be one of the pivotal events in the history of Middle-Earth.

Chapter Five: Riddles in the Dark
Bilbo seems hopelessly lost in the goblin-infested catacombs beneath the Misty Mountains. However, it is here that the

reader begins to see the value of Bilbo's courage, wit, and pragmatic thinking. Up to this point in the narrative, Bilbo has mostly been a comic character, partaking in the adventure but not really cut out for it. In chapter five, he transforms from a comic presence to a heroic one, a change that will occur over the rest of the story and for the rest of his life in Tolkien's later Middle-Earth tales. As Tolkien writes, "It was a turning point in his career, but he did not know it." (76)

What prompts or causes this change in Bilbo? Throughout the narrative, Gandalf has been hinting that there was more to Bilbo than his initial presence suggests. Thus, one possible answer is that by finding himself alone, lost, and in danger, Bilbo finally finds a reason to assert his heroic qualities that he would otherwise repress. Another possible reason for this change in Bilbo's character is that, while he is lost in the dark, Bilbo finds a magic gold ring. The ring, it turns out, is a very special object. Bilbo's possessing of the ring could also be the source of his alteration, changing him from a quiet hobbit into a daring hero. The ring factors in all the heroic actions Bilbo undertakes in *The Hobbit*, so there is textual evidence to support this theory. While the ring will have significant import to the action related in *The Lord of the Rings*, in *The Hobbit*, two central facts about the object emerge: It can make Bilbo invisible and, before Bilbo found it, the ring belonged to Gollum.

Tolkien introduces Gollum to the reader: "Deep down here by the dark water lived old Gollum, a small slimy creature. . . . He was Gollum—as dark as darkness, except for two big round pale eyes in his thin face . . . he was looking out of his pale lamp-like eyes for blind fish, which he grabbed with his long fingers as quick as thinking. He liked meat too." (80) While Gollum will emerge as one of the central characters in *The Lord of the Rings*, in *The Hobbit* he primarily plays the role of the first danger Bilbo must overcome on his own. As soon as Gollum hears Bilbo, he sneaks up on Bilbo, declaring, "'bless us and splash us, my precious! I guess it's a choice feast; at least a tasty morsel it'd make us, Gollum!' And when he said *Gollum* he made a horrible swallowing noise in his throat. That is how he got his name, though he always called himself my precious." (80)

Bilbo, faced with a slimy creature that wants to eat him, draws his sword, warning Gollum that it was made by elves many years ago. Gollum, not wanting to fight a sword-swinging hobbit, despite his desire to eat the hobbit, proposes a game of riddles. If Bilbo wins, Gollum will show him the way out of the catacombs; if Gollum wins, he gets to eat Bilbo. Throughout the game, both Bilbo and Gollum know some of the answers, while both also answer with very lucky guesses. Luck seems to play a large role in chapter five and emerges as a key theme. Here, luck is more properly considered in terms of *good fortune* or *providence*. These terms imply that something lucky happened but that the luck was the result of something more than blind chance. (Gandalf will explicate this idea in the closing passages of the last chapters of the book.) Fortune or providence suggests that there is a reason why something lucky has happened, perhaps even a "higher power" operating on behalf of and looking out for Bilbo or a sense of Bilbo's pre-scribed destiny having a hand in shaping these events.

This analysis can lead the reader to ponder the involve-ment of Bilbo in all these worldly events. On his own, it seems unlikely that Bilbo would have decided to go adventuring to unknown places, yet as a result of Gandalf knocking on his door one morning, that is where he ends up. Why did Gandalf pick Bilbo? Was Bilbo just a random selection, or did Gandalf have a deeper reason for selecting Bilbo? Is this an example of Bilbo's fate, his destiny?

Eventually, Bilbo wins the riddle game by "accidentally" asking the winning question. Fortune can be seen in the depic-tion of this event: "Bilbo pinched himself and slapped himself; he gripped his little sword; he even felt in his pocket with his other hand. There he found the ring he had picked up in the passage and forgotten about. 'What have I got in my pocket?' he said aloud. He was talking to himself, but Gollum thought it was a riddle."(87) Gollum is unable to answer this question, and Bilbo wins the riddle game. However, Gollum's treach-erous character reveals itself as he still plans on tricking Bilbo and eating him, despite promising not to if Bilbo won the game. Gollum, telling Bilbo he needs to retrieve something before he can show Bilbo the way out, returns to his cave to look for his "precious." However, the precious, which is what Gollum calls the ring, is missing, as it is in Bilbo's pocket. Gollum makes the connection between the missing ring and Bilbo's last riddle and flies into an uncontrollable, murderous rage. Bilbo, sensing the rage in Gollum's voice, begins to look for a way out of Gollum's cave:

> He put his left hand in his pocket. The ring felt very cold as it quietly slipped on to his groping forefinger. The hiss was close behind him. He turned and saw Gollum's eyes like small green lamps coming up the slope. Terrified he tried to run faster, but suddenly he struck his toes on a snag in the floor and fell flat with his little sword under him. In a moment Gollum was on him. But before Bilbo could do anything . . . Gollum passed by, taking no notice of him (92).

This passage raises several significant considerations. First, Tolkien reveals how Bilbo learned of the power of the ring to make him invisible; second, he raises the question of agency and the ring. Note that Tolkien wrote that the ring "quietly slipped on to" Bilbo's finger. The sentence implies that Bilbo did not consciously decide to put the ring on his finger but that it possibly decided to put itself on his finger. Consider also the use of the word *quietly*. Why note that a ring quietly slipped on to a finger. Do rings normally make noise when put on or off a finger? Quietly, in this context, can imply acting in a sneaky, or undetected manner. It seems, from Tolkien's prose, that the ring has agency. Note this characteristic of the ring and try to detect if, in other scenes depicting it, the ring seems to act as if it has a will of its own. Another point to consider is if this characteristic of the ring alters or has any bearing on the themes of fate and luck suggested earlier in this chapter.

Bilbo, wearing the ring, follows Gollum up the winding passages to escape. Bilbo escapes the clutches of Gollum, but as Gollum's closing speech indicates, the rivalry between Gollum and the Baggins clan is far from over: "Thief, thief, thief!

Baggins! We hates it, we hates it, we hates it for ever!" (96) Although this is Gollum's last appearance in *The Hobbit*, his hatred of the hobbits will fuel much of the action of *The Lord of the Rings*.

Having escaped from Gollum and the deepest realms of the mountains, Bilbo still needs to sneak by the goblins guarding the exit. When reading Tolkien's description of Bilbo's encounter with the goblin guards, note the developing relationship between the will of Bilbo and the will of the ring:

> They saw him sooner than he saw them. Yes they saw him. Whether it was an accident, or a last trick of the ring before it took a new master, it was not upon his finger. With yells of delight the goblins rushed upon him. A pang of fear and loss, like an echo of Gollum's misery, smote Bilbo, and forgetting even to draw his sword he struck his hands into his pockets. And there was the ring still, in his left pocket, and it slipped on his finger. He had vanished. (98)

Why did Tolkien compare Bilbo and Gollum at this point?

Chapter Six: Out of the Frying Pan into the Fire

The chapter opens with a reunion of Bilbo, Gandalf, and the dwarves. Bilbo tells them about his adventures in the lowest depths of the mountains and details his encounter with and escape from Gollum. However, Bilbo "forgets" to tell the group about the ring. This omission may prompt the reader to ask, was suppressing the discovery of such an object really accidental? Did Bilbo or the ring decide to conceal the identity of its possessor?

The party resumes its journey, but the adventurers soon discover that they have not yet escaped from the evil of the goblin army living in the Misty Mountains. A pack of wargs (evil wolves that work alongside goblins to spread terror and war throughout the countryside) attacks the party. The group tries to escape the wargs by climbing trees, but they only succeed in trapping themselves, as the wargs, joined by goblins, circle the trees and begin trying to roust the dwarves. Gandalf uses magic to kill some of the wargs, but the number of evil creatures increases so rapidly that he fears he cannot kill them all before the party is overrun.

This scene reveals elements of the state of nature as portrayed in Tolkien's fiction. For Tolkien, nature is not simply an inert, neural thing but a force that may be aligned with other good or evil forces. Some locales, such as Rivendale, propagate good, while others, such as Mirkwood (see chapter twenty), promote evil and act to hurt the characters. Likewise, Tolkien's natural world is not without its sensory abilities; it can hear and communicate with the people who inhabit it. Almost all animals can hear and speak, and most are organized into kingdoms much like the people of Middle-Earth are. In this chapter, the evil wargs and their chief are contrasted by the positive force of the eagles and their noble lord. Tolkien describes the balance:

> Eagles are not kindly birds. Some are cowardly and cruel. But the ancient race of the northern mountains were the greatest of all birds; they were proud and strong and noble hearted. They did not love Goblins, or fear them. When they took any notice of them at all . . . they swooped on them and drove them shrieking back to their caves, and stopped what ever wickedness they were doing. The goblins hated the eagles and feared them. (114)

Chapter Seven: Queer Lodgings

The adventurers take leave of the eagles and continue on their journey east to the Lonely Mountain. Gandalf informs the dwarves that he has pressing business elsewhere and cannot accompany them on their journey much longer. Before leaving, Gandalf introduces the party to Beorn, a magical being who lives in a cabin in the middle of the wilds. He is able to transform from a man into a bear, and in his bear form he travels his lands, protecting the animals that live there.

In addition to his wondrous ability to shape-shift, Beorn is also an emblem of Tolkien's ecological concerns. The natural world is almost always presented as something to be treasured and preserved in Tolkien's fiction, and Beorn acts as a type of ecological guardian in *The Hobbit*. Tolkien writes that Beorn "keeps cattle and horses which are nearly as marvelous as himself. They work for him and talk to him. He does not eat them; neither does he hunt or eat wild animals." (127) Beorn is a hermit and generally does not enjoy company. This provides an opportunity for Gandalf to use his wit to devise a humorous plan for Beorn to accept the dwarves into his home. Beorn finds Gandalf's plan and the party's behavior charming and witty, and he welcomes them into his home, extending them full hospitality. Again, we see that in Tolkien's world, social skills such as wit and charm are as valuable as sorcery and swordsmanship.

The group discovers that Beorn has a special hatred of goblins, because they defile the environment and are cruel to animals. When he learns of the death of the Great Goblin, he rewards the party with food and supplies for the rest of their journey and gives them two pieces of advice about trying to cross Mirkwood: They should not drink any water found in the forest and should never leave the path that crosses Mirkwood. He hints that doing either would lead to destruction. As the party prepares to enter Mirkwood, Gandalf departs, reminding them of Beorn's warning: "Don't leave the path." (152)

Chapter Eight: Flies and Spiders

The setting of this chapter merits closer analysis. Mirkwood is a huge forest, almost massive beyond belief. When looking at the maps Tolkien provides with *The Hobbit*, the forest seems to be the largest natural obstacle in the realm, even wider and longer than the mountain ranges. Following Tolkien's method, Mirkwood is an area inclined to evil. Whether this is because the forest itself is evil or because of the evil creatures that dwell there is not specified. The dreaded Necromancer lives in the woods, as do various other monsters. Mirkwood is described as a spooky, haunted place, full of potential pitfalls:

> There were black squirrels in the wood. As Bilbo's sharp inquisitive eyes got used to seeing things he could catch glimpses of them whisking off the path and scuttling

behind tree trunks. There were queer noises too, grunts, scufflings, and hurryings in the undergrowth, and among the leaves that lay piled endlessly thick in places on the forest floor; but what made the noises he could not see. The nastiest things they saw were the cobwebs: dark dense cobwebs with threads extraordinarily thick . . . it was not long before they grew to hate the forest as heartily as they had hated the tunnels of the goblins, and it seemed to offer even less hope of any ending. (154)

As the chapter continues, the forest becomes more and more claustrophobic, and the spirits of the party increasingly sink into gloom. After what seems like weeks of hiking through Mirkwood, the group finds its way barred by a sinister-looking river. Following Bilbo's advice, the party is able to cross the river, but calamity strikes as Bombur falls into the river during the crossing. The dwarves are able to pull him out of the water, yet he has already fallen victim to its spell: "When they laid him on the bank he was already fast asleep . . . and fast asleep he remained in spite of all they could do"(159). The dwarves are not able to rouse Bombur from his enchanted sleep, and they are forced to carry him as they follow the path. Of course, Bombur is the fattest of the dwarves, so their progress is slow.

Having failed to heed the first bit of Beorn's advice, it is not long before the party makes the erroneous decision to disregard the second bit of his advice: Do not leave the path. Pushed by hunger and fatigue, the party arrives at a desperate decision. They keep seeing what appear to be torches and campfires off the path deep in the woods. Curious, the group leaves the path and sneaks up on the fires. The camp, to their surprise, is a group of elves enjoying a cookout in the forest, but as soon as the dwarves are discovered, the fire is immediately extinguished and the elves disappear. The campfires keep reappearing, however, a little deeper in the woods, yet each time the dwarves approach, the fires again are snuffed out. Finally, after the fires have disappeared yet again, Bilbo hears the dwarves getting in trouble and calling for help, but he is unable to find them.

What is the potential significance of the fires in this scene? In one sense, they can be seen as a will-o'-the-wisp, a light that leads lonely travelers into a trap. Are the elves real? If so, why do they not stay to help Bilbo and the dwarves? Are these elves to be considered dangerous because of where they live? Elves are generally among the best-natured people of Middle-Earth, yet they are living in one of its regions most closely aligned with evil. Are these elves able to transform their environment for the better, or does their environment change them for the worse? A reader considering these questions may want to consult Tolkien's brief depiction of the wood elves and how they differ from the elves of Rivendale.

Bilbo, miserable at being alone again, sits down and begins to brood and taunt himself with thoughts of breakfast back in his warm, comfortable hobbit hole. While he ruminates, a giant spider sneaks up on him and tries to capture him in a web. Bilbo reacts instinctively and quickly kills the spider. For the second time, the reader sees Bilbo's heroic character emerge.

> There was the usual dim grey light of the forest day about him when he came to his senses. The spider lay dead beside him and his sword blade was stained black. Somehow the killing of the giant spider, all alone by himself in the dark without the help of the wizard or the dwarves or of anyone else made a great difference to Mr. Baggins. He felt a different person, and much fiercer and bolder in spite of an empty stomach, as he wiped his sword on the grass and put it back in its sheath. "I will give you a name," he said to it, and "I shall call you Sting." (170)

Bilbo, emboldened by his heroic killing of the giant creature, begins to look for his friends. He finds them, but they have been successfully captured by the spiders and are hanging upside down from a tree, cocooned in webs. The spiders greatly outnumber Bilbo, but he still decides to risk his life to rescue his friends. Again, this decision raises the consideration of whether this heroic action is something native to Bilbo's character or is the result of Bilbo being thrust into a heroic situation. Bilbo the spider slayer stands in sharp contrast to the figure Bilbo presented in the early chapters of the novel. Compare the Bilbo of the forest, charging a multitude of spiders with his sword Sting, to the Bilbo of chapter one, where he was more concerned with baking cakes and cleaning dishes than with combat.

After a long and well-orchestrated battle, Bilbo's strategy proves successful, and he rescues the dwarves and leads their escape. Bilbo seems more like a grim warrior than a hobbit, as he "darted backwards and forwards, slashing at spider threads, hacking at their legs, and stabbing at their fat bodies if they came too near. The spiders swelled with rage, and sputtered and frothed, and hissed out horrible curses; but they had become mortally afraid of Sting." (179) Tolkien ends the combat by describing the new Bilbo: "Bilbo began to feel there really was something of the bold adventurer about himself after all, though he would have felt a lot bolder still, if there had been anything to eat." (181) Tolkien masterfully retains Bilbo's loveable, humorous qualities, even after he has proved himself to be a warrior. As soon as the fight is over, Bilbo's hobbit nature reasserts itself.

The dangers of Mirkwood are many, however, and even though the party escaped from the spiders, they are still lost deep in the wood, having strayed far from the path. The weary dwarves discover that Thorin is missing, and they fear the worst. Although the dwarves suspect they have lost Thorin forever, Tolkien concludes the chapter by revealing that Thorin has been captured by the wood elves and is locked in the dungeon of the elf king.

Chapter Nine: Barrels out of Bond

The dwarves are captured by the wood elves and brought before the wood elf king. Bilbo uses his ring to avoid capture and follows the elves and their prisoners back to the king's cave. As is typical of elvish communities, the cave city is majestic, clean, and rather homely. The king asks the dwarves why they are wandering around Mirkwood. They refuse to tell him, so he orders them held in his prison. Tolkien makes sure to inform the reader that the elves took good care of their prisoners and tend to their well-being.

Bilbo, alone again, uses his ring to remain hidden "for a weary long time." (188) Bilbo takes advantage of his invisibility to explore the elf king's palace, eventually locating the prison cells of the dwarves. Bilbo, using his knowledge of the palace, develops a rescue plan. During a rather festive gathering, when all the elves are celebrating and getting drunk, Bilbo frees the dwarves from their cells. Bilbo's escape plan is a good example of his pragmatic thinking, as it would not be possible for the dwarves to break out of the palace by force or to sneak by the elves, whether the elves are drunk or not. Bilbo's creative solution is to hide the dwarves in barrels and then push the barrels into a river, letting them float away from the elf king's palace to the edge of the forest. Bilbo's solution is notable, as it demonstrates his intelligence and avoids the necessity for a confrontation with the wood elves.

As the journey and its dangers continue, the dwarves' attitude toward Bilbo begins to change. At first, the dwarves thought Bilbo a silly fool, a useless burden on the adventure. As the journey proceeds, and after Bilbo was able to use his wits (or courage or magic ring) to save the dwarves time and time again, the dwarves start to view Bilbo quite differently. They now see him as a successful burglar and adventurer and constantly turn to him for advice. They respect him and treat him as an equal. This is important to note, because this attitude will provide a sharp contrast to the dwarves' behavior after they have found the treasure and succumbed to gold lust.

Chapter Ten: A Warm Welcome

The dwarves and Bilbo float down the river until it empties into Long Lake at the foot of the human city of Lake-town. This community is inhabited by the descendants of the people who used to live in harmony with the dwarves of the Lonely Mountain many years ago, before the dragon Smaug took up residence there. The people of Lake-town still know of the legends of the King under the Mountain and, when they discover Thorin and the dwarves, they rejoice, believing that the dwarves have returned and that the riches of the Lonely Mountain will again spread throughout the land. The town's people welcome the dwarves, allowing them to rest and recuperate, and then resupplying them for their final assault on the dragon.

Chapter Eleven: On the Doorstep

Bilbo and the dwarves have reached the end of their journey, yet the most dangerous part of their adventure remains: defeating the dragon Smaug. The group is demoralized, as they realize they do not have a definite plan for fighting Smaug. Eventually they find the ledge where the secret door into the mountain is located, but they have no idea how to open the door. An elderly thrush appears and refuses to leave. Bilbo, ever perceptive, takes a hint from the thrush and uncovers the secret keyhole, enabling Thorin to unlock the door. As is becoming a recurring pattern in the novel, Bilbo has again proved his worth.

Chapter Twelve: Inside Information

The dwarves declare that it is time for Bilbo to "earn his reward" and sneak into the dragon's lair and steal something. Bilbo rightly answers that he has already earned his share but slips on his magic ring and descends down the secret passageway. The passage leads directly to the main lair of Smaug: "There he lay, a vast red-golden dragon, fast asleep; a thrumming came from his jaws and nostrils, and wisps of smoke, but his fires were low in slumber. Beneath him, under all his limbs and huge coiled tail, and about him on all sides stretching away across the unseen floors, lay countless piles of precious things, gold wrought and unwrought, gems and jewels, and silver." (233)

The dragon's hoard is impressively vast, and Bilbo is spellbound by the treasure. Regaining his senses, he steals a golden cup and runs back up the passage to the ledge where the dwarves are waiting for him. The dwarves are overjoyed at Bilbo's accomplishment, yet their joy does not last long, as they can hear the dragon awaken. Dragons apparently are not so easy to steal from after all: "Dragons may not have much real use for all their wealth, but they know it to an ounce as a rule, especially after a long possession, and Smaug was no exception. . . . There was a breath of fresh air in his cave. . . . He stirred and stretched forth his neck to sniff. Then he missed the cup! Thieves! Fire! Murder! Such a thing had not happened since he first came to the mountain!" (236)

Tolkien describes the dragon almost as a force of nature, as if the treasure is an extension of his identity or physical being, and his violent reaction to a single missing cup is like the angry defense of an animal guarding its lair. Tolkien will continue to play with natural imagery as he describes Smaug over the next few chapters, comparing him to thunder or an earthquake. In his rage, the dragon flies out of his lair, drenching the entire mountainside in flames. The adventurers are only able to survive by hiding from the dragon in the secret passage. Eventually the dragon tires and returns to his golden bed to set a trap for the thief. The dwarves are perplexed about what to do next, and Bilbo, having already proved himself to be a hero, proves himself to be a strong leader as well. He decides to don his ring and spy on the dragon to see if Smaug has any weaknesses. "Naturally the dwarves accepted the offer eagerly. Already they had come to respect little Bilbo. Now he had become a real leader in their adventure." (240)

Bilbo sneaks down the tunnel and finds what he thinks is a sleeping dragon. Smaug, however, is pretending to be asleep in order to catch the thief, and it is only because Bilbo is invisible that he is spared. Since Smaug can smell but not see Bilbo, the dragon engages him in conversation in an attempt to capture him. During this encounter, Bilbo again effectively mixes courage and pragmatism. He is courageous enough to spy on the dragon but not foolhardy enough to reveal himself to Smaug when the dragon pretends to welcome him into his lair. Bilbo and Smaug enter into a battle of wits, and each is able to gain something from the other. Smaug is able to trick Bilbo into revealing the existence of the dwarves, but more importantly, Bilbo is able to trick Smaug into showing him his belly. Bilbo flatters Smaug, who, responding, turns over to show off his jewel-encrusted underside, while simultaneously allowing Bilbo to discover Smaug's one weakness: "The dragon rolled over. 'Look!' he said. 'What do you say to that?' 'Dazzlingly marvelous! Perfect! Flawless! Staggering!' exclaimed Bilbo aloud, but what he thought inside was: 'Old fool! Why there is a large patch in the hollow of his left breast as bare as a snail out of its shell.'" (246) Bilbo, flush from outsmarting the dragon, ventures a joke at the dragon's expense, and Smaug responds by blasting his chamber with fire. Bilbo is barely able to escape.

Back outside, Bilbo tells the dwarves everything he has learned, especially about Smaug's weakness. The same thrush that helped Bilbo find the keyhole on the secret door seems to be listening intently to his report. Thorin notices the thrush and explains that the thrushes were a noble race of birds that lived in harmony with the residents of the mountain and valley before the dragon came. He also reveals that these thrushes can speak. The thrushes' verbal abilities are another example of how Tolkien presents the natural world as full of intelligent, knowledgeable creatures. The animals of Middle-earth have their own cultures, languages, and histories and, as such, are as integral to the world as humans are.

As Thorin begins to recall the legends of the treasure of the Lonely Mountain, he obsesses on one artifact in particular: the Arkenstone. While Thorin recalls the wonder of the Arkenstone, the party heads back into the passage for safety—and just in time, it turns out, as Smaug has emerged from the mountain, full of rage, and with plans to kill everything and everyone he can find. He blasts the mountain with fire, destroying the secret door, and heads off into the night, belching flames.

Chapter Thirteen: Not at Home

Suspense and tension mark this chapter as the dwarves are trapped inside the mountain and inside the dragon's lair. The dwarves wait in fear, expecting the dragon to return any moment and destroy them. Despite their anxious vigil, however, the dragon does not return. Instead, the dwarves start to reveal another aspect of their character, as the lure of the treasure outweighs any fear they have of the dragon, and they begin to explore the dragon's hoard.

The dwarves outfit themselves with armor and weapons, and Bilbo comes across another important object: the Arkenstone. He finds the legendary stone but does not tell the dwarves about it. Rather, he quietly puts it in his pocket: "Now I am a burglar indeed . . . but I suppose I must tell the dwarves about it—some time." (257) For now, Bilbo keeps his secret. Why does he withhold such information, as it seems out of character for him? Has he fallen victim to treasure lust? After all the accusations from Gollum and Smaug, has he really become a thief? Or was Bilbo's finding of the Arkenstone yet another example of his fate or destiny as a powerful guiding force in his story?

Chapter Fourteen: Fire and Water

This chapter reveals why the dragon did not return to kill the dwarves. After destroying the secret door, Smaug flew to Lake-town, trailing death as he went. Smaug attacks the town, causing mayhem and destruction. He would have succeeded in killing everyone, except for a small band of warriors who stood their ground and fought the dragon. This group was led by one grim warrior named Bard, who refuses to flee. In a climactic scene, Bard and the dragon do battle:

> But there was still a company of archers that held their ground among the burning houses. Their captain was Bard, grim voiced and grim faced . . . he was a descendant in a long line of Girion, Lord of Dale . . . now he shot with a great yew bow till all his arrows but one were spent . . . suddenly, out of the dark, something fluttered to his shoulder. He started—but it was only an old thrush. Unafraid it perched by his ear and brought him news. Marveling he found he could understand its tongue, for he was of the race of Dale. (270)

The thrush tells Bard of the dragon's one weak spot, the lone unarmored spot on his chest. Bard draws his last arrow, a magical black one, which had been a gift to his family from the last King under the Mountain, ages before Smaug appeared.

The dragon swooped once more lower than ever, and as he turned and dived down his belly glittered white with sparkling fires of gems in the moon—but not in one place. The great bow twanged. The black arrow sped straight from the string, straight for the hollow by the left breast . . . In it smote and vanished, barb shaft and feather . . . with a shriek that deafened men, felled trees and split stone, Smaug shot spouting into the air, turned over, and crashed down from on high in ruin. (270)

The death of Smaug cannot be fully celebrated, however, as Lake-town has been destroyed in the battle and the surviving residents left destitute. They call for Bard, the dragon slayer, to become King Bard and lead them to rebuild their community. The Master of Lake-town attempts to beguile the crowd into keeping him as leader, revealing only his desire for personal power and wealth over the general good of the people. While the people of Lake-town are trying to make survival plans, an elvish army, led by the elf king of the forest, appears.

The elf king and his army, having heard about the death of the dragon, quickly set out to claim a share of the treasure as their own. Being elves, they are able to move quickly and appear on the scene almost instantaneously. Their speed, it turns out, proves a boon for the surviving people of Lake-town, as the elves share their food and shelter with the humans. Again, Tolkien wants to demonstrate that the elves, led by their king, and the humans, led by Bard, are good beings who are simply laying claim to what they believe is their justified share of the treasure. Bard and the surviving warriors of Lake-town agree to join with the elf king and march on Lonely Mountain.

With the claims the elves and the humans make on their share of the dragon's treasure, Tolkien wants to depict the elves and humans as driven not by greed alone but motivated by actual need. Bard notes that Smaug destroyed Lake-town (and that he had preyed on the lake men for years) and that the humans will need money if they are to survive and rebuild their town. The elves likewise claim that Smaug had stolen some of the treasure from the elves and that his presence had negatively impacted their kingdom. Are these respective claims justified and honorable, or are they an attempt to take part of the treasure by force? Are these demands in or out of character? How does the reader anticipate Thorin's reply?

Chapter Fifteen: The Gathering of the Clouds

As chapter fifteen opens, Bilbo and the dwarves are continuing their inventory of the dragon's treasure, when they are interrupted by the old thrush and a raven. The birds tell the dwarves about the death of Smaug and the approaching army of men and elves. The birds tell Thorin that Bard is a just and honorable leader and that the armies only seek their fair share. Thorin and the dwarves are in the grip of treasure lust and can think of little besides protecting all the gold. They send the raven to bring the news to Thorin's cousin Dain, a leader of a kingdom of dwarves in the Iron Hills, and to ask him to send an army of dwarves to help defend the treasure. They then set about fortifying the mountain.

After several days, the army of elves and men appear before the mountain, and Bard, the elf king, and Thorin hold a meeting. Bard presents his claim, and Thorin quickly dismisses it. Finally, Bard sends a herald to the gate of the mountain:

> In the name of Esgaroth and the Forest, one cried, we speak unto Thorin Thrain's son Oakenshield, calling himself King under the Mountain, and we bid him consider well the claims that have been urged, or be declared our foe. At the least he shall deliver one twelfth portion of the treasure unto Bard, as the dragon slayer and as the heir of Girion. From that portion Bard will himself contribute to the aid of Esgaroth; but if Thorin would have the friendship and honor of the lands about, as his sires had of old, then he will give also somewhat of his own for the comfort of the men of the lake. (287–88)

Tolkien makes one last effort to depict the claim of Bard, as the slayer of the dragon, as justified and reasonable, as Bard offers to use his own share of the treasure to help rebuild the town. He also appeals to Thorin's sense of charity, to donate a tiny amount of his gold to help his poor and starving people. Tolkien makes Bard's last offer inarguably reasonable in order to highlight the unreasonableness of Thorin's refusal. Thorin, tragically, is no longer acting reasonably, as he has fallen victim to treasure lust as well.

Chapter Sixteen: A Thief in the Night

The raven and thrush return to tell Thorin that Dain has answered his call and has led an army of dwarves from the Iron Hills to the Lonely Mountain. Thorin rejoices at this news, but the birds plead with Thorin to forgo war and to strike a truce with Bard. Thorin rejects this sound counsel. Why, however, do the birds keep asking Thorin to avoid battle? Since the birds are not dwarves, they are immune to the treasure lust that besets Thorin and his party. This desire to avoid bloodshed also allows Tolkien one last chance to demonstrate the essential goodness of the people involved in this struggle over the gold and, more importantly, allows the author to justify Bilbo's next action.

Bilbo, as a hobbit, is not as strongly affected by the treasure as the dwarves are and is able to see the logic and justice in the claims presented by Bard. Likewise, he is peaceful by nature and does not want to see three races—elves, dwarves, and humans—fight one another in a battle. Finally, Bilbo is afraid that the coming battle will cause some of his friends to lose their lives, dying in a meaningless and unnecessary war.

To avoid this catastrophe, Bilbo comes up with a daring plan. He puts on his ring and, taking the Arkenstone with him, sneaks out of the mountain and down into the joint human-elvish camp. Bilbo tries to make a deal with Bard and the elf king, telling them he is willing to divide his personal share of the treasure with the men and elves of Lake-town, as long as that would prevent a war. To proves his trustworthiness, Bilbo gives them the Arkenstone to use as ransom for his share of the treasure. Bard and the elf king declare Bilbo to be a good and honorable hobbit and agree to his deal. Bilbo announces that he will return to his friends the dwarves, because in his mind he was not betraying them but simply trying to stop a fight among those who should be otherwise peaceable. As Bilbo is leaving Bard's camp, he is approached by an old man: "'Well done! Mr Baggins!' he said, clapping Bilbo on the back. 'There is always more about you than anyone expects.' It was Gandalf"(295).

Chapter Seventeen: The Clouds Burst

Dain and his army have reached the mountain, and the prospects for peace look bleak. Bard approaches the mountain and makes one final negotiation to attempt to avoid war. Following Bilbo's plan, Bard reveals that he has the Arkenstone and will return it to the dwarves in exchange for Bilbo's share of the treasure. When Thorin hears of Bilbo's plan, he curses Bilbo and declares him an enemy for life. Not even Gandalf can change Thorin's mind:

> "By the beard of Durin! I wish I had Gandalf here! Curse him for his choice of you! May his beard wither! As for you I will throw you to the rocks!" he cried and lifted Bilbo in his arms.
>
> "Stay! Your wish is granted!" said a voice . . . "Here is Gandalf! And none to soon it seems. If you don't like my burglar please don't damage him. Put him down and listen to what he has to say!"
>
> "You all seem in league!" said Thorin dropping Bilbo on the top of the wall. "Never again will I have dealings with any wizard or his friends. What have you to say, you descendant of rats?"
>
> "Dear me!" said Bilbo . . . "You may remember saying that I might choose my own fourteenth share? Perhaps I took it too literally. I have been told that dwarves are sometimes politer in word than in deed. The time was, all the same, when you seemed to think that I had been of some service. Descendant of rats, indeed! Is this all the service of you and your family that I was promised? Take it that I have disposed of my share as I wished, and let it go at that!" (297–98)

This exchange between Bilbo, Thorin, and Gandalf offers rich interpretive opportunities. First, it allows the reader to see how greatly the treasure lust has affected Thorin, drastically altering his character. After all that Bilbo has done over the course of the narrative, it is easy to see that Thorin's attack on Bilbo is unjustified, and his rejection of his old friend Gandalf is unfair. It also reveals how generally good-natured and fair-minded hobbits are and how pointless some wars are.

Thorin continues to reject Bard's offer and everyone's advice to make a peaceful settlement. Battle seems unavoidable, and the armies of dwarves, humans, and elves prepare for combat. The battle is just about to start when Gandalf magically appears between the armies: "in a voice like thunder, and his staff blazed forth with a flash like the lightning. "Dread has come upon you all! Alas! it has come more swiftly than I guessed. The Goblins are upon you . . . They ride upon wolves and Wargs are in their train!" (302)

Earlier in the novel, when the party had been captured in the Misty Mountains by goblins, they killed the Great Goblin and many of his tribe during their escape. In the meantime, while the party was journeying through Mirkwood and eventually to the Lonely Mountain, the goblins had sworn revenge and amassed a large army made up of all the goblin tribes of the wild. This goblin army now appears before the Lonely Mountain, eager and bloodthirsty. Sensing their doom, the elves, dwarves, and humans listen to Gandalf and form an alliance to fight the goblin army. Yet even aligned, their army pales in size to the mass of assembled goblins. The armies engage each other, which Tolkien describes as "a terrible battle." (305)

Bilbo, invisible because of his ring, takes refuge as the battle rages around him all day. It is a long and bloody skirmish, and despite the valor of the heroes of the story, by the end of the day it seems as if the numbers of the goblin army are too great and that everyone will be "slaughtered or driven down and captured" (308). At the last moment, when it seems the goblins are just about to be victorious, a cry rings out across the battlefield: ""The Eagles! The Eagles!" he shouted. 'The Eagles are coming!'" (308) As Bilbo looks to the skies, a rock strikes him on the head, and he falls unconscious.

Chapter Eighteen: The Return Journey

Bilbo is alive, and the goblins have been defeated. A soldier finds Bilbo, who has removed the ring, and takes him to a tent where Bard and an injured Gandalf are waiting for him. Gandalf leads Bilbo farther into the tent, where a sad sight awaits him. Thorin has been wounded in the battle and is on the verge of death. On his deathbed, Thorin apologizes for his treatment of Bilbo before the battle and makes his final speech in the narrative: "'No!' said Thorin. 'There is more in you of good than you know, child of the kindly West. Some courage and some wisdom, blended in measure. If more of us valued food and cheer and song above hoarded gold, it would be a merrier world. But sad or merry, I must leave it now. Farewell.'" (312)

Thorin's dying words warrant a closer look. First, the gold lust has lost its grip on Thorin, as he loses his grip on life. Yet Thorin realizes the error of his ways, since the dragon died, and makes peace with Bilbo, thus cementing the friendship between the characters that had developed over the course of the narrative. Thorin's words also introduce a new value system to the world, a system in which hospitality and generosity are valued above gold and precious stones. Finally, Tolkien reveals something of the deeper character of hobbits as emblems of goodness in the history of Middle-earth.

After Thorin dies, Gandalf tells Bilbo about how the battle ended. The arrival of the eagles slowed down the progress of the goblin army, but it was the surprise appearance of another old friend that turned defeat into victory. Beorn, in the form of a giant bear, appeared "no one knew how or from where. He came alone and in bear's shape, and he seemed to have grown almost to giant-size in his wrath." (313) Again victory over evil comes from the efforts of many good people, of various shapes and abilities, joining together and fighting as one.

Dain, as a blood member of the dwarven royal family, becomes King under the Mountain. Heeding the lessons of the battle, he divides the wealth fairly, giving treasure to Bard, to the elf king, and to provide for the rebuilding of the human city of Dale. Dain becomes a just king, and Bard proves to be a noble king of Dale, the men and dwarves of the valley living in harmony. Gandalf and Bilbo gather a portion of their share of the treasure and set out on the long voyage back to Bilbo's home, as Bilbo was getting tired of adventures and only thought of his comfortable armchair back in his warm hobbit hole.

Chapter Nineteen: The Last Stage

Bilbo and Gandalf retrace their steps on their journey home, stopping first in Rivendale, where the reason for Gandalf's departures at various moments in the text is revealed. Gandalf and other wise and powerful wizards and elf lords had waged war on the Necromancer, chasing him out of his dark tower in Mirkwood. While this information does little in *The Hobbit* but fill in some gaps in the story, it will prove to be a central event in *The Lord of the Rings*. Bilbo also recovers the hidden troll treasure, left behind by the party at the beginning of the adventure.

Finally, Bilbo returns home. However, in a scene foreshadowing Frodo's return at the end of *The Lord of the Rings*, Bilbo arrives to find that he has been declared dead and his home and possessions put up for auction. He also discovers that he has lost more than some possessions; he has also lost his reputation. "For ever after he remained an elf-friend, and had the honor of dwarves, wizards, and all such folk . . . but he was no longer quite respectable. He was in fact held by all the hobbits of the neighborhood to be 'queer,' except by his nephews and nieces on the Took side." (327)

Obviously, Bilbo has become a heroic character, a friend of the wise and powerful, and has proved himself to be a good, just, and peace-loving person. Yet the people of his hometown do not consider those facts when they think of him. For them, all that matters is that he is different now, and, to them, different is bad, undesirable. Tolkien is obviously commenting on the unhealthy conservatism of close-minded people. Yet the broader point remains; once individuals make a decision to leave the safe, traditional, and well-known enclaves behind to embrace and experience life, life changes them. Living is a process of growth that involves embracing the new, and the rewards of life are only earned by those who take the chance of living it.

The final dialogue between Gandalf and Bilbo, which closes the novel, provides the last point of discussion for *The Hobbit* and complements the earlier discussions of Tolkien, Bilbo, and destiny. Bilbo, after looking back with wonder on his adventure, declares, "'Then the prophecies of the old songs have turned out to be true, after a fashion!'" (330) Gandalf replies:

> "And why should not they prove true? Surely you don't disbelieve the prophecies, because you had a hand in bringing them about yourself? You don't really suppose, do you, that all your adventures and escapes were managed by mere luck, just for your sole benefit? You are a very fine person, Mr. Baggins, and I am very fond of you, but you are only quite a little fellow in a wide world after all!" (330).

Tolkien leaves the reader to ponder on the mix of destiny and agency in the adventures of Bilbo Baggins and, by doing so, enfolds the narrative into a longer, grander narrative of history and the role that individuals, no matter how small they seem, may play in it.

Critical Views

KATHARYN W. CRABBE ON
THE QUEST AS FAIRY TALE

In 1937 Tolkien's first book, *The Hobbit*, appeared on the children's lists of Allen and Unwin. It was an immediate success as a children's book, receiving consistently good reviews, though it made no impression at all on the adult market. Like the fairy tales to which it is closely akin, it was thought to be appropriate only for the nursery, though many reviewers noted that the ideal reader of the adventures of Bilbo Baggins would have to be imaginative, intelligent, and an excellent reader. In writing *The Hobbit*, Tolkien had reasonable success in doing what he attempted to do, but what he attempted to do was neither complex nor ambitious. The plot is simple and linear; the characters tend to be all good or all bad; and the central issue—the battle between good and evil—is clearly drawn and clearly resolved. That is, *The Hobbit* lacks complexity in conception, in design, and in execution. Its simplicity and its obviously having been written down to a naive audience make it far less interesting and much less an artistic achievement than *The Lord of the Rings*, though the two works share many themes and some characters.

Critics who feel driven to identify the stylistic qualities that mark *The Hobbit* as a children's book characteristically point to the avuncular asides that appear throughout the narrative. In such asides as, "It was just at this moment that Bilbo suddenly discovered the weak point in his plan. Most likely you saw it some time ago and have been laughing at him; but I don't suppose you would have done half so well yourselves in his place," they argue, the narrator not only intrudes on his own story by stepping into the narrative frame and addressing the readers directly, he is also coy and talks down to his readers. This much is probably true, as Tolkien repudiated his narrative stance in *The Hobbit* within a very short time after it was published, saying, "*The Hobbit* was written in what I should now regard as bad style, as if one were talking to children. There's nothing my children loathed more. They taught me a lesson. Anything that was in any way marked out in *The Hobbit* as for children, instead of just for people, they disliked—instinctively. I did too, now that I think about it." However, there are other less exceptionable practices in language use that as clearly mark *The Hobbit* as a book intended for the young or the naive reader. These are narrative characteristics which serve to illustrate for the reader how literature is to be read, that is, how details of action or description may be used as the basis for inference.

Take, for example, the problem of characterization. One learns early on in *The Hobbit* that qualities of character may be surmised by looking closely at the kind of language the character uses. So Bilbo's description of Gandalf's fireworks, "They used to go up like great lilies and snapdragons and laburnums of fire and hang in the twilight all evening," tells us something of the way his mind works. But the narrator feels obliged to help his reader draw that inference—"You will notice already that Mr. Baggins was not quite so prosy as he liked to believe."

Similarly, the narrator does not quite trust his reader to see or appreciate the significance of Bilbo's decision to go down the tunnel to the treasure trove of Smaug. Though the description of the rumble and throb of Smaug's snoring creates a sense of a hell fire waiting below, and though Bilbo's reluctance to enter the tunnel has been made clear, the narrator adds, "Going on from there was the bravest thing he ever did. The tremendous things that happened afterward were as nothing compared to it. He fought the real battle in the tunnel, alone, before he saw the danger that lay in wait." Now, there is nothing wrong with these descriptions or with the others like them throughout the book. They are not exactly condescending in tone, nor are they really stylistically inappropriate. But they assume a very naive reader, one incapable of drawing inferences or understanding symbolic meaning. They assume, that is, a child.

There are, as well, other language choices and attitudes that show Tolkien was writing *The Hobbit* for a young audience and was manipulating the language in appropriate ways for such a group. For example, the narrator assumes that the reader will not be able to find his way around in any organization more complicated than straight chronology. Thus he feels obliged to take his reader by the hand when he does anything sophisticated, such as using a flashback. So, when chapter 13 ends with Bilbo and the dwarves wondering what happened to Smaug, chapter 14 begins by answering the question: "Now if you wish, like the dwarves, to hear news of Smaug, you must go back again to the evening when he smashed the door and flew off in a rage, two days before." That is as tidy an example of steering a naive reader through a transition that makes use of a sophisticated narrative device as one can imagine.

It is then quite sure that *The Hobbit* is a children's book, in the sense that it was written with a childish or naive reader in mind. But it does not logically follow, as many critics seem to assume, that the book is unworthy of critical attention. Though Tolkien later repudiated the technique of *The Hobbit*, he could not (and would not have wanted to) deny that the work still reflects the workings of his remarkably fertile mind, and that, though the themes are treated in such a way as to be accessible to children, they have enough significance and enough subtlety of development to reward the attentive adult. Like other fairy tales, *The Hobbit* is thematically concerned with the human situation, not simply with childish ones.

Hobbits, the avuncular narrator tells us, are little people, about half our height. They have brown curly hair on their heads and on their feet, though they do not have beards. They are good-natured and sociable, appreciating their food and their tobacco (which they call pipeweed) and preferring brightly colored clothes, particularly vests. They are very shy outside their own territory and, consequently, are almost never seen by "the big folks," as they call us. Whenever they hear one of the big folks coming, they steal away silently through the fields and woods of the Shire, the region of Middle-earth where they live.

The hobbit is Bilbo Baggins, who, as he is sitting down to tea one day, hears adventure knocking at his door. Thirteen dwarves, led by Thorin, son of Thráin, King Under the Mountain, have decided to return to the Lonely Mountain of their ancestors to reclaim the treasure stolen from them by Smaug the Dragon. For reasons Bilbo does not understand, the wizard Gandalf has chosen him to accompany the dwarves and to help them to recover the treasure. *The Hobbit* is the story of Bilbo's adventures with the dwarves, his role in recovering the treasure, and his return to his comfortable hobbit hole.

Thematically, *The Hobbit* is primarily concerned with increasing maturity. As Bilbo travels with the dwarves through adventures with trolls, goblins, and giant spiders, he changes from a frightened, passive, ineffectual lover of domestic comfort to a brave, realistic, active planner of events who is willing to take responsibility for himself and others.

After being almost eaten by trolls (who are luckily outsmarted by Gandalf), almost murdered by goblins, threatened by a strange underground creature called Gollum (from whose lair comes a magical ring that makes the wearer invisible), rescued by eagles, and captured by giant spiders and then by Wood-elves, the adventurers finally reach the Lonely Mountain. Here Bilbo asserts his leadership and finds the treasure, awakening the dragon's wrath in the process. When the rampaging dragon is killed by one of the men who live along the lake at the base of the mountain, the dwarves think their claim to the treasure is clear. However, men and elves soon appear to claim a share, and war threatens to break out. Bilbo steals the Arkenstone, the most famous and most beautiful gem of the hoard, and gives it to the men to use as a lever against Thorin's claim of the whole treasure. In doing so, he hopes to avert a disaster. His effort fails, however, and men, dwarves, and elves are saved from shedding one another's blood only by the attack upon all of them by the goblins and Wargs who wish to avenge the losses they suffered at the hands of Thorin and Company earlier.

When the battle is over, Bilbo knows the bitterness and joy of heroic involvement in life. He returns home, quite a new hobbit, both shunned and honored for his unusual involvement in adventures: "He took to writing poetry and visiting the elves; and though many shook their heads and touched their foreheads and said 'Poor old Baggins!' and though few believed any of his tales, he remained very happy to the end of his days, and those were extraordinarily long." One could hardly ask for a more classic fairy-tale ending.

Having said that *The Hobbit* is a book much akin to a fairy tale, it would perhaps be a good idea to consider that statement for a moment: What are the characteristics associated with fairy tales? Fairy tales are stories that take place in a secondary world—a world in which nature is alive in a nearly human way, and the laws that govern man and nature are not the same as those of the world we occupy. Thus, in the world of a fairy tale, animals may talk, magic may happen, people may come back to life, or live for extraordinarily long expanses of time. The heroes of fairy tales tend to be the small and the weak—youngest brothers or sisters, for example, or people who are thought to be dullards. But they have virtues that allow them to overcome the strong and the powerful—a good nature, or a streak of kindness, or an amazing cunning quickness. In fairy tales, good and evil tend to be presented in black and white, although the distinction is more likely to be made on the basis of what the hero needs psychologically than what the laws of religion or property teach us. For example, in "Jack the Giant Killer," it is far more important to Jack's story that he out-smart the giant and his wife than that the rights of property be respected, that is, that the giant retain possession of his golden harp. The giant is clearly bad because he tries to keep Jack from existing as an individual (by eating him), and in the eyes of the fairy tale that is a more important crime than Jack's theft, which is part of his growing up.

BRIAN ROSEBURY ON THE NOVEL AS A TRANSITIONAL WORK IN TOLKIEN'S DEVELOPMENT

Tolkien's first published work of fiction is in many respects a dry run for *The Lord of the Rings*, though Tolkien of course did not conceive it as such, and it is scarcely a fifth of the length of the later work. Its hero Bilbo, like Frodo, is a hobbit who becomes, only half-voluntarily, engaged in a quest: the recapture of dwarves' treasure, stolen by the dragon Smaug, who now hoards it in the Lonely Mountain far off in the East. After a leisurely opening at Bilbo's home in Hobbiton, the narrative is dominated by the journey to the Mountain (a series of largely unconnected adventures), until in the final third of the tale several of its threads come together in a relatively complex political and moral entanglement. The dragon, aroused by the intrusion of Bilbo and the dwarves, is killed after devastating a nearby community of men, Lake-Town: and the competing claims of dwarves, Lake-men and elves for compensation from his hoard are fairly recognised only by Bilbo, who smuggles the dwarves' priceless Arkenstone into the Elvenking's camp to be used in bargaining. An attack by goblins (the 'orcs' of *The Lord of the Rings*) unites the disputing parties just as war seems on the point of breaking out. The dwarves' leader, Thorin Oakenshield, is mortally wounded in the battle, and forgives the 'traitor' Bilbo before dying.

'Farewell, good thief,' he said. 'I go now to the halls of waiting to sit beside my fathers, until the world is renewed. Since I leave now all gold and silver, and go where it is of little worth, I wish to part in friendship from you, and I would take back my words and deeds at the Gate.'

Bilbo knelt on one knee filled with sorrow. 'Farewell, King under the Mountain!' he said. 'This is a bitter adventure, if it must end so; and not a mountain of gold can amend it. Yet I am glad that I have shared in your perils—that has been more than any Baggins deserves.'

'No!' said Thorin. 'There is more in you of good than you know, child of the kindly West. Some courage and some wisdom, blended in measure. If more of us valued food and cheer and song above hoarded gold, it would be a merrier world. But sad or merry, I must leave it now. Farewell!'

Then Bilbo turned away, and he went by himself, and sat alone wrapped in a blanket, and whether you believe it or not, he wept until his eyes were red and his voice was hoarse. He was a kindly little soul. (*The Hobbit*, p. 243)

As the close of this extract suggests, *The Hobbit* is somewhat too consciously conceived as a children's book: 'whether you believe it or not' is typical of the fireside intimacies to which the narrative is prone (and which Tolkien later regretted), and the deliberately *naif* diction and syntax of this and the final sentence seems to wrap Bilbo in a blanket of paternal tenderness. The anti-acquisitive moral, too, is spelt out more carefully and repeatedly than an adult reader, or possibly any reader, needs. (These shortcomings are further proof that the 1938 essay 'On Fairy Stories', with its vigorous rejection of any necessary association between children and fairy-tales, represents a turning-point in Tolkien's thinking.) Yet one reason that Thorin's words about food and cheer are superfluous is that the situation has a realistic moral tension that requires no underlining. Bilbo has betrayed the dwarves for good reasons—because Thorin's obstinacy in defending the entire hoard threatens futile slaughter—and their prior debt to him is much greater than his to them, but he has nevertheless betrayed them, and Thorin's rage has been understandable. Bilbo's remark about his own deserts is a sufficient, though oblique, apology for his 'treachery'; Thorin repents his covetousness, and each forgives the other. The dialogue is effective because (as the occasion surely demands) the forgiveness is expressed with a minimum of explicit reference to the events which have divided them: Thorin's 'good thief' initiates this blend of bluntness and indirection. (The allusion to the Gospels which some readers will discern in these words is, so to speak, optional, or accidental: the phrase describes Bilbo quite literally, especially as he has been explicitly engaged by the dwarves as a 'burglar'.) The style of both characters' declarations is at once elevated and laconic, close to that of many dialogue passages in *The Lord of the Rings* in which the hobbits or other speakers adapt their normal discourse to a formal or solemn occasion. The success of the episode depends upon the reader's willingness to concentrate on the thoroughly-imagined situation, to allow it to validate the momentarily dignified language, and to extend a certain indulgence to the lapses into sententiousness or chattiness. Indeed, this is true of the whole work.

Catherine Stimpson calls it 'a genial, attractive book. . . . The whole narrative has the lilt and zest of fresh inspiration'. But for Tolkien's hostile critics, patting *The Hobbit* on the head has become something of a tradition: the critic indicates a benevolent receptiveness towards 'fantasy' (when confined to the marginal world of children's books) before proceeding to ridicule the ambitious scale and implied adult readership of *The Lord of the Rings*. It seems to me that, on the contrary, *The Hobbit* is very uneven in inspiration, and flawed by inconsistencies of tone and conception; that it is essentially a transitional work, a stopping-off point on Tolkien's creative journey from the rudimentary forms of bedtime story-telling to the richly 'realistic' narrative of *The Lord of the Rings*, a journey that converges in that work with the progressive abandonment of the mannered archaism of the early mythical writings. So far from being an accomplished success 'on its own level', *The Hobbit* is an uneasy, if likeable, patchwork of accomplishments, blunders, and tantalising promises of the Middle-earth to come.

At one level, its most characteristic, *The Hobbit* functions extremely effectively as an adventure story for children that makes no particular bid for internal realism, or for emotional or moral depth. The delightful opening chapter, in which Bilbo is simply selected out of the blue as the burglar for the dwarves' expedition, makes no attempt to disguise the *deus ex machina* role of Gandalf in getting the adventure started. The thirteen dwarves' arrival at Bag End, in unannounced groups at more or less regular intervals, is a stylised effect (a kind of burlesque of the iterative structure of fairy-tale) which Tolkien is not above repeating several chapters later. Bilbo's wild shriek of terror at Thorin's remark that 'all of us . . . may never return' (p. 23) is a piece of comic business rather than a psychologically credible response. Several subsequent episodes, such as the encounter with three ill-bred trolls, or the battle with spiders, whom Bilbo taunts with insulting names, are gripping enough in a Disney-cartoon sort of way, but leave no impression of a serious encounter with evil: the villains lack a moral history or distinctive motive, and the forces of good triumph through superior guile, energy and luck. Each conflict is essentially a battle of wits. Even Bilbo's confrontation with Gollum by his underground pool—rewritten for the 1951 second edition, to harmonise with *The Lord of the Rings*—is maintained at this stylised level by the ritual of the Riddle-Game the two characters play. Towards the end, as we have already seen, the story modulates into a more serious key. But it concludes with a conventional and unambiguous happy ending: Bilbo returns to Bag End enriched, with memories and with gold. He has lost nothing, except his spoons and his reputation for respectability.

At times *The Hobbit* falls below, or rises above, this level. The dialogue is often under-differentiated, with figures such as Thorin and Gandalf lapsing intermittently into a bourgeois banality more appropriate to Bilbo. There are occasional narrative contrivances which revision could easily have disguised, as when Dori tells Gandalf several things he knows already— 'All of a sudden you gave one of your blinding flashes . . . You shouted "Follow me everybody!"' (p. 84)—for the benefit of an eavesdropping Bilbo and an eavesdropping reader. The humour sometimes cuts against, rather than functioning within, the integrity of the fictional 'history': there is, for example, a particularly incongruous and laboured joke about the invention of golf (p. 24). The notion of 'magic', largely avoided in *The Lord of the Rings* in favour of a putatively consistent system of powers and 'lore', is too often invoked (sometimes in the vaguest terms) in the evident hope of lending colour to a prosaic episode or passage.

On the other hand, we find from the very beginning glimpses of an exhilarating temporal and spatial scope. The fifty-year-old Bilbo, we learn in the first chapter, 'had apparently settled down immovably' at Bag End. Then, 'by some curious chance one morning long ago in the quiet of the world, when there was less noise and more green . . . Gandalf came by' (p. 13). Both sentences imply the untroubled enjoyment of wide expanses of time, an impression reinforced by the prolonged, seemingly inconsequential conversation that follows.

'Good morning!' said Bilbo, and he meant it. The sun was shining, and the grass was very green. But Gandalf looked at him from under long bushy eyebrows that stuck out further than the brim of his shady hat.

'What do you mean by that?' he said. 'Do you wish me a good morning, or mean that it is a good morning whether I want it or not; or that you feel good this morning; or that it is a morning to be good on?'

'All of them at once,' said Bilbo. 'And a very fine morning for a pipe of tobacco out of doors, into the bargain. If you have a pipe about you, sit down and have a fill of mine! There's no hurry, we have all the day before us!' Then Bilbo sat down on a seat by his door, crossed his legs, and blew out a beautiful grey ring of smoke that sailed up in the air without breaking and floated away over the Hill. (*The Hobbit*, p. 13)

As for space, Bilbo 'loved maps, and in his hall there hung a large one of the Country Round with all his favourite walks marked on it in red ink' (p. 26). The many windows of Bag End overlook Bilbo's garden 'and meadows beyond, sloping down to the river' (p. 11). For Bilbo and his neighbours the features of the local landscape are simply 'The Hill', 'The Water', 'The Country Round': beyond them is the wide blue yonder into which only the reckless venture.

Tolkien is, of course, in this opening chapter building a land of heart's desire by elaborating the fairy-tale formula 'once upon a time', and adopting the perspective formed in childhood (but deeply embedded in adult consciousness) of the world as concentric circles centred upon Home. As he observes in 'On Fairy Stories',

If a story says, 'he climbed the hill and saw a river in the valley below' . . . every hearer of the words will have his own picture, and it will be made out of all the hills and rivers and dales he has ever seen, but specially out of The Hill, The River, The Valley which were for him the first embodiment of the word.

The insight is not especially original. What is important is the conviction with which the compositional project is carried out. Through writing *The Hobbit*, initially for his own children, Tolkien discovered not only the hobbit's-eye-view which humanised (if one can put it that way) his mythical vision in *The Lord of the Rings*, but also the concretely imagined Middle-earth of the later work, though he did not yet call it by that name and though its realisation was as yet rudimentary. The two qualities are in fact connected: the hobbits' grateful and unassuming pleasure in life, which gathers value and significance as the narratives of *The Hobbit* and *The Lord of the Rings* proceed, requires the texture of experience to be evoked as compellingly as possible. That in turn requires a plain and transparent, but flexible and sensuously alert, prose style. The simple and direct, even at times naive and homespun, style of *The Hobbit* was an indispensable rehearsal for the huge narrative labour of *The Lord of the Rings*. The 'old castles with an evil look, as if they had been built by wicked people' which Bilbo sees on the 'dreary hills' of the Lone-lands (p. 34) may represent only the faintest inkling of Isengard or the tower of Minas Morgul; but in phrases and sentences a paragraph later the mature style can be seen beginning to emerge.

Humphrey Carpenter on Bilbo Baggins

[Tolkien's] deep feeling that his real home was in the West Midland countryside of England had, since his undergraduate days, defined the nature of his scholarly work. The same motives that had led him to study *Beowulf*, *Gawain*, and the *Ancrene Wisse* now created a character that embodied everything he loved about the West Midlands: Mr Bilbo Baggins, the hobbit.

We can see certain superficial precedents for this invention: the Snergs, the name Babbitt, and in Tolkien's own stories the original four-foot Tom Bombadil and the tiny Timothy Titus. But this does not tell us very much. The personal element is far more revealing. In the story, Bilbo Baggins, son of the lively Belladonna Took, herself one of the three remarkable daughters of the Old Took, descended also from the respectable and solid Bagginses, is middle aged and unadventurous, dresses in sensible clothes but likes bright colours, and has a taste for plain food; but there is something strange in his character that wakes up when the adventure begins. John Ronald Reuel Tolkien, son of the enterprising Mabel Suffield, herself one of the three remarkable daughters of old John Suffield (who lived to be nearly a hundred), descended also from the respectable and solid Tolkiens, was middle aged and inclined to pessimism, dressed in sensible clothes but liked coloured waistcoats when he could afford them, and had a taste for plain food But there was something unusual in his character that had already manifested itself in the creation of a mythology, and it now led him to begin this new story.

Tolkien himself was well aware of the similarity between creator and creation. 'I am in fact a hobbit,' he once wrote, 'in all but size. I like gardens, trees, and unmechanized farmlands; I smoke a pipe, and like good plain food (unrefrigerated), but detest French cooking; I like, and even dare to wear in these dull days, ornamental waistcoats. I am fond of mushrooms (out of a field); have a very simple sense of humour (which even my appreciative critics find tiresome); I go to bed late and get up late (when possible). I do not travel much.' And as if to emphasise the personal parallel, Tolkien chose for the hobbit's house the name 'Bag End', which was what the local people called his Aunt Jane's Worcestershire farm. Worcestershire, the county from which the Suffields had come, and in which his brother Hilary was at that time cultivating the land, is of all West Midland counties The Shire from which the hobbits come; Tolkien wrote of it: 'Any corner of that county (however fair or squalid) is in an indefinable way "home" to me, as no other part of the world is.' But the village of Hobbiton itself with its mill and river is to be found not in Worcestershire but in Warwickshire, now half hidden in the red-brick skirt of Birmingham but still identifiable as the Sarehole where Ronald Tolkien spent four formative years.

The hobbits do not owe their origins merely to personal parallels. Tolkien once told an interviewer: 'The Hobbits are just rustic English people, made small in size because it reflects the generally small reach of their imagination—not the small reach of their courage or latent power.' To put it another way, the hobbits represent the combination of small imagination with great courage which (as Tolkien had seen in the trenches during the First World War) often led to survival against all chances. 'I've always been impressed,' he once said, 'that we are here, surviving, because of the indomitable courage of quite small people against impossible odds.'

In some ways it is wrong to talk of hobbits as the 'missing piece' that was needed before the two sides of Tolkien's imagination during the nineteen-twenties and thirties could meet and fuse; at least chronologically wrong, because Tolkien probably began to write *The Hobbit* quite early in this period. It would be more accurate to say that not until the book was finished and published—indeed not until he began to write the sequel—did he realise the significance of hobbits, and see that they had a crucial role to play in his mythology. In itself *The Hobbit* began as merely another story for amusement. Moreover it nearly suffered the fate of so many others and remained unfinished.

While we can see quite clearly why Tolkien began to write the story, it proves impossible to say exactly when. The manuscript gives no indication of date, and Tolkien himself was unable to remember the precise origins of the book. In one account he said: 'I am not sure but I think the Unexpected Party (the first chapter) was hastily written before 1935 but certainly after 1930 when I moved to 20 Northmoor Road.' Elsewhere he wrote: 'On a blank leaf I scrawled "In a hole in the ground there lived a hobbit". I did not and do not know why. I did nothing about it, for a long time, and for some years I got no further than the production of Thror's Map. But it became *The Hobbit* in the early nineteen-thirties.' This recollection that there was a hiatus between the original idea and the composition of the main body of the story is confirmed by a note that Tolkien scribbled on a surviving page of the original Chapter One: 'Only page preserved of the first scrawled copy of *The Hobbit* which did not reach beyond the first chapter.' In 1937, shortly after the book was published, Christopher Tolkien recorded (in his letter to Father Christmas) this account of the book's origins: 'Daddy wrote it ages ago, and read it to John, Michael and me in our Winter "Reads" after tea in the evening; but the ending chapters were rather roughly done, and not typed out at all; he finished it about a year ago.' And writing to his publishers during the same year, Tolkien declared: 'My eldest boy was thirteen when he heard the serial. It did not appeal to the younger ones who had to grow up to it successively.'

These statements lead to the conclusion that the book was begun in 1930 or 1931 (when John, the eldest boy, was thirteen); certainly there was a completed typescript in existence (lacking only the final chapters) in time for it to be shown to C. S. Lewis late in 1932. However John and Michael Tolkien do not believe this to be the entire picture, for they have a clear memory of certain elements in the story being told to them in the study at 22 Northmoor Road, that is, before 1930. They are not certain that what they were listening to at that time was necessarily a *written* story: they believe that it may well have been a number of impromptu tales which were later absorbed into *The Hobbit* proper.

The manuscript of *The Hobbit* suggests that the actual writing of the main part of the story was done over a comparatively short period of time: the ink, paper, and handwriting style are consistent, the pages are numbered consecutively, and there are almost no chapter divisions. It would also appear that Tolkien wrote the story fluently and with little hesitation, for there are comparatively few erasures or revisions. Originally the dragon was called 'Pryftan', the name 'Gandalf' was given to the chief dwarf, and the wizard was called 'Bladorthin'. The dragon's name was soon changed to 'Smaug', from the Germanic verb *smugan* meaning 'to squeeze through a hole'; Tolkien called this 'a low philological jest'. But the name 'Bladorthin' was retained for some time, and it was not until the draft was well advanced that the chief dwarf was renamed

'Thorin Oakenshield' and the name 'Gandalf' (taken, like all the dwarf-names, from the Elder Edda) was given to the wizard, for whom it was eminently suitable on account of its Icelandic meaning of 'sorcerer-elf' and hence 'wizard'.

The story began, then, merely for personal amusement. Certainly Tolkien had at first no intention that the bourgeois comfortable world of Bilbo Baggins would be related in any way to the vast mythological landscape of *The Silmarillion*. Gradually, however, elements from his mythology began to creep in. Inevitably the dwarves suggested a connection, for 'dwarves' (spelt in that fashion) had played a part in the earlier work; and when in the first chapter of *The Hobbit* the wizard mentioned 'the Necromancer' there was a reference to the legend of Beren and Lúthien. Soon it was apparent that the journey of Bilbo Baggins and his companions lay across a corner of that Middle-earth which had its earlier history chronicled in *The Silmarillion*. In Tolkien's words this was 'the world into which Mr Baggins strayed'. And if the events of the new story were clearly set long after those of *The Silmarillion*, then, since the earlier chronicles recorded the history of the First and Second Ages of Middle-earth, it appeared that *The Hobbit* was to be a tale of the Third Age.

'One writes such a story,' said Tolkien, 'out of the leaf-mould of the mind'; and while we can still detect the shape of a few of the leaves—the Alpine trek of 1911, the goblins of the 'Curdie' books of George Macdonald, an episode in *Beowulf* when a cup is stolen from a sleeping dragon—this is not the essential point of Tolkien's metaphor. One learns little by raking through a compost heap to see what dead plants originally went into it. Far better to observe its effect on the new and growing plants that it is enriching. And in *The Hobbit* the leaf-mould of Tolkien's mind nurtured a rich growth with which only a few other books in children's literature can compare.

For it is a children's story. Despite the fact that it had been drawn into his mythology, Tolkien did not allow it to become overwhelmingly serious or even adult in tone, but stuck to his original intention of amusing his own and perhaps other people's children. Indeed he did this too consciously and deliberately at times in the first draft, which contains a large number of 'asides' to juvenile readers, remarks such as 'Now you know quite enough to go on with' and 'As we shall see in the end'. He later removed many of these, but some remain in the published text—to his regret, for he came to dislike them, and even to believe that any deliberate talking down to children is a great mistake in a story. 'Never mind about the young!' he once wrote. 'I am not interested in the "child" as such, modern or otherwise, and certainly have no intention of meeting him/her half way, or a quarter of the way. It is a mistaken thing to do anyway, either useless (when applied to the stupid) or pernicious (when inflicted on the gifted).' But when he wrote *The Hobbit* he was still suffering from what he later called 'the contemporary delusions about "fairy-stories" and children'—delusions that not long afterwards he made a conscious decision to renounce.

The writing of the story progressed fluently until the passage not far from the end where the dragon Smaug is about to die. Here Tolkien hesitated, and tried out the narrative in rough notes—something he was often to do in *The Lord of the Rings* but seems to have done only rarely in *The Hobbit*. These notes suggest that Bilbo Baggins might creep into the dragon's lair and stab him. 'Bilbo plunges in his little magic knife,' he wrote. 'Throes of dragon. Smashes walls and entrance to tunnel.' But this idea, which scarcely suited the character of the hobbit or provided a grand enough death for Smaug, was rejected in favour of the published version where the dragon is slain by the archer Bard. And then, shortly after he had described the death of the dragon, Tolkien abandoned the story.

Or to be more accurate, he did not write any more of it down. For the benefit of his children he had narrated an impromptu conclusion to the story, but, as Christopher Tolkien expressed it, 'the ending chapters were rather roughly done, and not typed out at all'. Indeed they were not even written in manuscript. The typescript of the nearly finished story, made in the small neat typeface of the Hammond machine, with italics for the songs, was occasionally shown to favoured friends, together with its accompanying maps (and perhaps already a few illustrations). But it did not often leave Tolkien's study, where it sat, incomplete and now likely to remain so. The boys were growing up and no longer asked for 'Winter Reads', so there was no reason why *The Hobbit* should ever be finished.

*   *   *

One of the few people to be shown the typescript of *The Hobbit* was a graduate named Elaine Griffiths, who had been a pupil of Tolkien's and had become a family friend. Upon his recommendation she was engaged by the London publishers George Allen & Unwin to revise Clark Hall's translation of *Beowulf*, a popular undergraduate 'crib'. One day in 1936 (some time after *The Hobbit* had been abandoned) a member of Allen & Unwin's staff came down to Oxford to see Elaine Griffiths about the project. This was Susan Dagnall, who had read English at Oxford at the same time as Elaine Griffiths and indeed knew her well. From her she learnt of the existence of the unfinished but remarkable children's story that Professor Tolkien had written. Elaine Griffiths suggested that Susan Dagnall should go to Northmoor Road and try to borrow the typescript. Susan Dagnall went, met Tolkien, asked for the typescript, and was given it. She took it back to London, read it, and decided that it was certainly worthy of consideration by Allen & Unwin. But it stopped short just after the death of the dragon. She sent the typescript back to Tolkien, asking him if he would finish it, and preferably soon, so that the book could be considered for publication in the following year.

Tolkien got down to work. On 10 August 1936 he wrote: '*The Hobbit* is now nearly finished, and the publishers clamouring for it.' He engaged his son Michael, who had cut his right hand badly on a school window, to help with the typing, using his left hand. The whole labour was finished by the first week in October, and the typescript was sent to Allen & Unwin's offices near the British Museum, bearing the title *The Hobbit, or There and Back Again*.

The firm's chairman, Stanley Unwin, believed that the best judges of children's books were children, so he handed *The Hobbit* to his ten-year-old son Rayner, who read it and wrote this report:

> Bilbo Baggins was a hobbit who lived in his hobbit-hole and *never* went for adventures, at last Gandalf the wizard and his dwarves perswaded him to go. He had a very exiting time fighting goblins and wargs. at last they got to the lonley mountain; Smaug, the dragon who gawreds it is killed and after a terrific battle with the goblins he returned home—rich! This book, with the help of maps, does not need any illustrations it is good and should appeal to all children between the ages of 5 and 9.

The boy earned a shilling for the report, and the book was accepted for publication.

Despite what Rayner Unwin had written, it was decided that *The Hobbit* did need illustrations. Tolkien was modest about his talents as an artist, and when at the publishers' suggestion he submitted a number of drawings which he had made for the story he commented 'The pictures seem to me mostly only to prove that the author cannot draw.' But Allen & Unwin did not agree, and they gladly accepted eight of his black and white illustrations.

Although Tolkien had some idea of the processes involved in the production of books, he was surprised by the number of difficulties and disappointments during the following months; indeed the machinations and occasionally the downright incompetence of publishers and printers continued to amaze him until the end of his life. *The Hobbit* maps had to be redrawn by him because his originals had incorporated too many colours, and even then his scheme of having the general map as an endpaper and Thror's map placed within the text of Chapter One was not followed. The publishers had decided that both maps should be used as endpapers, and in consequence his plan for 'invisible lettering', which would appear when Thror's map was held up to the light, had to be abandoned. He also had to spend a good deal of time on the proofs—though this was entirely his fault. When the page-proofs arrived at Northmoor Road in February 1937 he decided that he ought to make substantial revisions to several parts of the book, for he had let the manuscript go without checking it with his usual thoroughness, and he was now unhappy about a number of passages in the story; in particular he did not like many of the patronising 'asides' to juvenile readers, and he also saw that there were many inconsistencies in the description of the topography, details which only the most acute and painstaking reader would notice, but which he himself with his passion for perfection could not allow to pass. In a few days he had covered the proofs with a host of alterations. With typical consideration for the printers he ensured that his revisions occupied an identical area of type to the original wording—though here he was wasting his time, for the printers decided to reset the entire sections that he had revised.

The Hobbit was published on 21 September 1937. Tolkien was a little nervous of Oxford reaction, especially as he was currently holding a Leverhulme Research Fellowship, and he remarked: 'I shall now find it very hard to make people believe that this is not the major fruits of "research" 1936–7.' He need not have worried: at first Oxford paid almost no attention.

A few days after publication the book received an accolade in the columns of *The Times*. 'All who love that kind of children's book which can be read and re-read by adults', wrote the reviewer, 'should take note that a new star has appeared in this constellation. To the trained eye some characters will seem almost mythopoeic.' The eye in question was that of C. S. Lewis, at that time a regular reviewer for *The Times Literary Supplement*, who had managed to get this notice of his friend's book into the parent journal. Naturally, he also reviewed the book in glowing terms in the *Supplement* itself. There was an equally enthusiastic reaction from many other critics, although some took a delight in pointing out the ineptness of the publisher's 'blurb' that compared the book to *Alice in Wonderland* simply because both were the work of Oxford dons; and there were a few dissenting voices, among them that of the reviewer who wrote (somewhat puzzlingly) in *Junior Bookshelf*: 'The courageous freedom of real adventure doesn't appear.'

The first edition of *The Hobbit* had sold out by Christmas. A reprint was hurried through, and four of the five coloured illustrations that Tolkien had drawn for the book were now included in it; he had apparently never offered them to Allen & Unwin, and it was not until they passed through the publisher's office on the way to Houghton Mifflin, who were to publish the book in America, that their existence was discovered. When the American edition was issued a few months later it too received approbation from most critics, and it was awarded the *New York Herald Tribune* prize for the best juvenile book of the season. Stanley Unwin realised that he had a children's best-seller in his list. He wrote to Tolkien: 'A large public will be clamouring next year to hear more from you about Hobbits!'

PERRY C. BRAMLETT ON
THE HOBBIT AS CHILDREN'S LITERATURE

Tolkien evidently did not have a high opinion of the *Hobbit*, particularly after its publication (1937) and during the time of his continued work on the *Silmarillion* and the writing and publishing of the *Lord of the Rings*. In a December 1937 letter to G. E. Selby he wrote: "I don't much approve of the *Hobbit* myself, preferring my own mythology . . . with its consistent nomenclature . . . and organized history . . . to this rabble of Eddaic-named dwarves . . ."[1] In later correspondence with W. H. Auden, Tolkien told the poet that the *Hobbit* was "unhappily meant" as a children's story and that it contained some of the "silliness" of certain children's books he had read in his childhood. And in a draft of a letter (April 1959, never sent) he said that the *Hobbit* was "published hurriedly and without due consideration," and was not addressed specifically to children as an audience, but came out of his made-up stories for his own children. He further added that the *Hobbit* was a "first essay or introduction" to the *Lord of the Rings*.[2]

And he remembered only some of its origins: "All I can remember about the start of the *Hobbit* is sitting correcting School Certificate papers in the everlasting weariness of that annual task forced on impecunious academics with children. On a blank leaf I scrawled: 'In a hole in the ground there lived a hobbit.'"[3] Tolkien could not remember exactly when he wrote these words, although once he said it was after 1930. But his eldest sons John and Michael remembered hearing parts of the story read to them and their younger brother Christopher by their father between 1926–1930, and Michael wrote imitation hobbit stories ("apocryphal Hobbitry") that he dated 1929. He later guessed that his father started writing the story sometime between the summer of 1928 and continued it into 1929. John later told the BBC that his father read to them parts of the story for several Christmases, and Christopher remembered hearing it read to the boys in their winter "reads" after tea in the evening.[4]

Enough of the story had been written by late 1932 or early 1933 that Tolkien showed it to C. S. Lewis. In an early 1933 letter to his friend Arthur Greeves, Lewis mentioned that he had delighted in reading it, that it was "good" except the end (Lewis's version did not have Tolkien's later added chapters), and that there was a question to whether or not the story would succeed with "modern children." Tolkien's former student Elaine Griffiths remembered Tolkien lending her an early typed copy of the *Hobbit*, and that she read it with "enormous pleasure" and thought it was wonderful. In 1936, when she worked for Allen & Unwin, Griffiths, while working on a translation of *Beowulf*, was visited in Oxford by her friend Susan Dagnall, who also worked for the publisher. Griffiths recommended the *Hobbit* to Dagnall, who met Tolkien and took a borrowed copy of the story back to London.

Dagnall read and approved the story, then returned it to Tolkien, suggesting that he finish it (the incomplete story ended with the death of the dragon) and submit it for publication in 1937. Tolkien finished the story in late September 1936, and sent it to Allen & Unwin on 3 October. Stanley Unwin gave the manuscript to his ten-year-old son Raynor for review, for the standard fee of one shilling. Young Rayner liked the story, and a sentence from his review is worth noting: "He (Bilbo Baggins) had a very exciting time fighting goblins and wargs. At last they got to the lonely mountain; Smaug, the dragon who gawreds it is killed and after a terrific battle with the goblins he returned home—rich!"[5] Rayner thought the story was "good," did not need any illustrations, and thought it would be enjoyed by all children between the ages of five and nine.

Allen & Unwin's production department had some difficulties with the five maps planned for the book, and after discussion with Tolkien, they asked him to design them, with two eventually being used, Thror's Map and the Wilder land (Marched) Map. After much discussion, many letters back and forth from Unwin and Tolkien, and several revisions, the British first edition of the *Hobbit* was published on 21 September 1937, with an initial printing of 1,500 copies, 150 of these review and sample copies. The book's complete title was the *Hobbit or There and Back Again Being the Record of a Years Journey Made by Bilbo Baggins of Hobbiton Compiled from his Memoirs*. It included "Thror's Map" (front endsheets), "Wilder land" (back endsheets), and ten additional illustrations by Tolkien: "The Hill: Hobbiton Across the Water," "The Trolls," "The Mountain-path," "The Misty Mountains Looking West from the Eyrie towards Goblin's Gate," "Beorn's Hall," "Marched" (color), "The Elvenking's Gate," "Lake Town," "The Front Gate," and "The Hall at Bag-End, Residence of B. Baggins Esquire." Tolkien also designed the dust jacket (with several revisions) and drew the designs for the cover, which included dragons, mountains, moon, runes, and sun.

Tolkien wrote a descriptive blurb for the British edition, and part of it read, "If you care for journeys there and back, out of the comfortable Western world, over the edge of the Wild, and home again, and can take an interest in a humble hero (blessed with a little wisdom and a little courage and considerable good luck), here is the record of such a journey and such a traveler . . . you will learn by the way . . . much about trolls, goblins, dwarves, and elves, and get some glimpses into the history and politics of a neglected but important period."[6]

He received his advance copy of the book on 13 August 1937, it was published on 21 September, and the first printing was sold out by 15 December. A second printing of 2,300 copies was released on 25 January 1938 and sold out quickly, although over 400 copies of these (in sheets) were destroyed in warehouse by Hitler's bombs. The first US edition was published by Houghton Mifflin (Boston) on 1 March 1938, by June nearly 3,000 copies had been sold, and by the end of 1938 over 5,000 copies had been sold.

By 1947 the British edition was in its fourth impression, by 1991 it was reported that annual sales had reached 100,000 copies, and the 1992 centenary printing of 80,000 copies was sold out before publication. Since 1937, and after the success of the *Lord of the Rings*, the *Hobbit* has been reprinted scores of times by several publishers, in paperback, anniversary, children's, special, "gift," and even comic editions, and estimates of its sales to the present day have approached fifty million copies worldwide. It has been translated into over twenty-five languages, including Swedish (the first, 1947), Hebrew, French, Estonian, Bulgarian, Japanese, and Dutch.

After Tolkien submitted his *Hobbit* manuscript to Allen and Unwin, an editor there complained about his spelling of "dwarves," and pointed out that the *OED* spelled it "dwarfs." Tolkien's reply was: "I *wrote* the *Oxford English Dictionary*!"[7] This must not have helped, because the first British paperback edition (Puffin, 1961) contained several notable misprints, including "dwarves" and "elvish" being changed to "dwarfs" and "elfish."[8] Ballantine (a Houghton Mifflin imprint), which published the first US paperback edition (1965), did not include Tolkien's revisions or consult him about the design of the dust jacket.

Most of the early reviews were good, with many reviewers comparing the *Hobbit* to Lewis Carroll's *Alice in Wonderland* and *Through the Looking-Glass*. C. S. Lewis reviewed the book twice anonymously, in the 2 October 1937 issue of the *Times Literary Supplement*, and in the 8 October 1937 issue of the *Times*. In the first review, he wrote that the *Hobbit* "may well prove to be a classic," and in the second he said that Tolkien had united several things, including humor, an understanding of children, and "a happy fusion of the scholar's with the poet's grasp of mythology." In the United States, Anne Eaton reviewed the *Hobbit* for the *New York Times Book Review* and *Horn Book Magazine* and said the work was "written with a quiet humor and the logical detail in which children take delight." William R. Bent, writing for *Saturday Review of Literature*, called the *Hobbit* "a gorgeous fancy." In May of 1938 the *New York Herald Tribune* awarded the book a $250 prize in an annual children's festival, calling it the best book published that spring for younger children. Sinclair Lewis's young son Michael (aged seven) called the *Hobbit* "an adorable story" (for an advertising blurb for Houghton Mifflin), and Tolkien provided a drawing of a hobbit for Houghton Mifflin's fall advertising push, which was printed in the Christmas edition of *Horn Book Magazine*.

Tolkien did not plan for the *Hobbit* to have a sequel. When the *Lord of the Rings* was nearing its completion in 1947, he understood that he would have to change the account of how Bilbo obtained the Ring, as in the original version the ring had magical powers but was not the Ring of Power, the One Ring. Tolkien then revised parts of chapter five of the *Hobbit* to show that Gollum planned to kill Bilbo from the beginning, and that his ring was the One Ring. This revised version was published in the second edition of the *Hobbit* in 1951, along with a note from Tolkien explaining that this version was "the true story" that Bilbo eventually told Gandalf. . . .

. . . In January 1938, the *London Observer* published a letter asking Tolkien to tell his readers more about hobbits and suggesting that he might have been influenced by an article by Julian Huxley, which described "little furry men" seen in Africa by natives and "at least one scientist." The letter also mentioned an old (1904) fairy tale called "The Hobbit," and asked if the cup-stealing scene in Tolkien's tale was from *Beowulf*. Tolkien responded with a long letter, explaining that he had no recollection from his reading about "furry pigmies" in Africa, nor of the hobbit fairy tale. He protested that his hobbits did not live in Africa, had fur only on their feet, and that the two hobbits in the *Observer* were "accidental homophones" (a word having the same sound as another but meaning something quite different). Tolkien went on to say that he did not remember anything about the name and inception of Bilbo (the hero), and that he would leave the game of guessing the origins of hobbits to "future researchers."[11] Years later, he told an interviewer that the word *hobbit* might have been derived from Sinclair Lewis's *Babbitt* (1922). Tolkien had evidently read the novel, as he commented that "Babbitt has the same bourgeois smugness that hobbits do."[12]

There have been several other theories about the origin of hobbits. In British folklore there are several examples of certain wraiths and elves called *hobs*, *hobthrusts* (a good-natured goblin or "local spirit, famous for whimsical pranks"), and *hobyahs*, while *hob* is an old word for "rustic" or "clown," and a *hoball* or *hoblob* or *hobbil* or *hob-hald* is a "clown" or "fool."[13] Tom Shippey mentioned a collection of folklore tales called the *Denham Tracts* that describe supernatural creatures, written by Michael A. Denham and edited by Dr. James Hardy, which were published in two volumes in 1892 and 1895. In volume two, the word *hobbit* is mentioned as a "class of spirit."[14] Tolkien's hobbits were certainly not "spirits," and he could have known about them from the Denham book, but we will probably never know. In 1977, a Tolkien journal stated that the *London Times* reported (6 May 1977) that the word *hobbit* had been found in a 1586 catalogue of "hobgoblins, boggarts, and other fantastic creatures."[15]

Notes

1. Christopher Tolkien, ed., *The Return of the Shadow* (Boston: Houghton Mifflin, 1988) 7.

2. Humphrey Carpenter, *The Letters of J. R. R. Tolkien* (London: Allen & Unwin, 1981) 297–98.

3. Ibid., 215.

4. Humphrey Carpenter puts the date in 1930 or 1931, stating that the version of the story the boys heard may have been have been oral, or "impromptu tales." See *J. R. R. Tolkien: A Biography* (Boston: Houghton Mifflin, 2000) 181. This was verified by Tolkien in a letter dated 16 July 1964, when he said he invented and told stories to his children and sometimes wrote them down. See Carpenter, *Letters*, 346.

5. Wayne G. Hammond, *J. R. R. Tolkien: A Descriptive Bibliography* (New Castle DE: Oak Knoll Books, 1993) 8.

6. Douglas A. Anderson, *The Annotated Hobbit* (Boston: Houghton Mifflin, 1988) 3.

7. Deborah Rogers quoted with approval an anecdote from Daniel Grotta-Kurska's usually unreliable biography (93). See Rogers, *Tolkien: A Critical Biography* (New York: Hippocrene Books, 1980) 20, 128. The 1933 edition of the *OED* (vol. 3, p. 732) defined *dwarf* as "one of a supposed race of diminutive beings, who figure in Teutonic and esp. Scandinavian mythology and folklore; often identified with the elves . . ."

8. This would happen to Tolkien again, with the publication of the *Lord of the Rings*.

11. See Carpenter, *Letters*, 30–32.

12. See Anderson, *Annotated Hobbit*, 5.

13. From the 1933 edition of the *Oxford English Dictionary*.

14. See Shippey, *J. R. R. Tolkien: Author of the Century* (London: HarperCollins, 2000) 3.

15. *Mythprint* 15/5 (June 1977): 1. *Mythlore* 16 (vol. 4, no. 4, June 1977) inside back page.

COLIN DURIEZ ON PHYSICAL AND SPIRITUAL JOURNEYS

On a summer's day around the end of the 1920s a slight man—indistinct in contrast to the brightness outside—sits by an open window at his desk, a pen in hand, a Toby Jug sprouting pipes and a wooden tobacco jar nearby. A slant of sun touches him. His hair is so fine that the light makes the crown of his head shine. The comparative gloom of the study is emphasized by an abundance of dark-bound books—books lining the walls of the room from floor to ceiling, books even creating the sides of a tunnel through which one enters the study, shelves protruding outwards on either side of the door. The man is silent, except for an occasional muttered "O lor," reluctantly concentrating upon the task in hand. For beside him are two piles of papers. The larger is made up of unmarked school certificate exam papers. The smaller pile is made up of the already marked ones. Abandoned sheets of elegant manuscript perch on the edge of the desk.

Tolkien, like Lewis, undertakes the seasonal task of grading papers to supplement his meager university income. Both have households to support. Tolkien would rather be working on his poetic version of "The Tales of Beren and Lúthien Elf-maiden," teasing out some detail of the chronology of the First Age of Middle-earth, or checking out the origin and formation in an Elven variant of the name of a particular character who has sprung, unbidden, into the story.

This particular summer's day seems likely to be uneventful, as many before it. There are the familiar sounds of his boys playing in the garden, and the undeniable mountain of scripts to be evaluated before his voluntary imprisonment is over. All changes, however, when Tolkien turns over a page and, instead of a hastily written answer, finds it blank. This is joy indeed. One of the candidates, mercifully it seems to him, has left one of the folios with no writing on it. Tolkien hesitates a moment, then inscribes boldly across the sheet: "In a hole in the ground there lived a hobbit." As always, names generate a story in his mind. Eventually he decides that he had better find out what these mysterious hobbits are like.

*   *   *

By late 1932 Tolkien was able to hand Lewis a sheaf of papers to read. It was the incomplete draft of what became *The Hobbit: or There and Back Again*. Lewis described his reaction to it in a letter to Arthur Greeves: "Reading his fairy tale has been uncanny—it is so exactly like what we would both have longed to write (or read) in 1916: so that one feels he is not making it up but merely describing the same world into which all three of us have the entry." Lewis had already written to Greeves in rosiest terms of his friendship with Tolkien, comparing it favorably with their own—like them, Lewis said, he had grown up on William Morris and George MacDonald. In a letter a few weeks later he mentions Tolkien sharing their love of "romance" literature, and in the same sense: "He agreed that for what *we* meant by romance there must be at least the hint of another world—one must hear the horns of elfland."

The Hobbit was eventually published on September 21, 1937, complete with Tolkien's own illustrations; the initial printing was fifteen hundred copies. W. H. Auden, when he reviewed *The Fellowship of the Ring* for the *New York Times* on October 31, 1954, wrote: "in my opinion, [*The Hobbit*] is one of the best children's stories of this century."

Though Tolkien probably began writing the book in 1930, his eldest sons, John and Michael, remembered the story being told to them before the 1930s. Perhaps various oral forms of the story merged into the more finished written draft. What is significant from these indistinct memories is that *The Hobbit* began as a tale told by a father to his children. It was consciously written as a children's story, and this fact shapes its style. It also seems that at first the story was independent of Tolkien's burgeoning mythological cycle, "The Silmarillion," and was only later incorporated into his invented world and history. The tale introduced hobbits into Middle-earth, dramatically affecting the course of events there. *The Hobbit* belongs to the Third Age of Middle-earth, and chronologically precedes *The Lord of the Rings*.

At the time of publication Lewis reviewed his friend's book for *The Times Literary Supplement*: "Prediction is dangerous: but *The Hobbit* may well prove a classic." Another critic, in the *New Statesman*, remarked of Tolkien: "It is a triumph that the genus *Hobbit*, which he himself has invented, rings just as real as the time-hallowed genera of Goblin, Troll, and Elf." Lewis believed that the hobbits "are perhaps a myth that only an Englishman (or, should we add, a Dutchman?) could have created." Instead of a creation of character as we find it in standard novels, much of the personality of Bilbo, Frodo, and Sam derives from their character as hobbits, just as we identify Gandalf in character as a wizard or Treebeard as an Ent. Tolkien sustains the collective qualities of these different mythological species with great skill.

The title of *The Hobbit* refers to its unlikely hero, Mr. Bilbo Baggins. He is a creature of paradox, summed up in his oxymoronic role as a bourgeois burglar in the story. Before Bilbo, hobbits aimed at having a good reputation with their peers—not only by being comfortably off, but by not having any adventures or doing anything unexpected. Bilbo's house was a typical dwelling place of a wealthy hobbit. It was not a worm-filled, dirty, damp hole, but a comfortable, many-roomed underground home. Its hall, which connected all the rooms, had "panelled walls, and floors tiled and carpeted, provided with polished chairs, and lots and lots of pegs for hats and coats—the hobbit was fond of visitors." Hobbits generally liked to be thought respectable, not having adventures or behaving in an unexpected way. They were lifted from Tolkien's childhood world of the rural West Midlands, the inspiration for The Shire.

Bilbo's reputation is tarnished forever when he is suddenly caught up in the quest for dragon's treasure. He reluctantly finds this more congenial than he ever thought. A whole new world is opened up to him, and in later years he even becomes somewhat of a scholar, translating and retelling tales from the older days. The quest also develops his character, though he always retains the quality of homeliness associated with hobbits and The Shire where they live.

In *The Hobbit* a party of dwarves, thirteen in number, are on a quest for their long-lost treasure, which is jealously guarded by the dragon, Smaug. Their leader is the great Thorin Oakenshield. They employ Bilbo Baggins as their master burglar to steal the treasure, at the recommendation of the wizard Gandalf the Grey. At first the reluctant Mr. Baggins would rather spend a quiet day with his pipe and pot of tea in his comfortable hobbit-hole than partake in any risky adventure.

But as their journey unfolds, the dwarves become increasingly thankful for the fact that they employed him, despite initial misgivings, as he gets them out of many scrapes. He seems to have extraordinary luck. At one point in the adventure Bilbo is knocked unconscious in a tunnel under the Misty Mountains, and left behind in the darkness by the rest of the party.

Reviving, Bilbo discovers a ring lying beside him in the tunnel. It is the ruling ring, the One Ring, that would eventually form the subject of *The Lord of the Rings*, but at this stage Bilbo is to discover only its magical property of invisibility. After putting the ring in his pocket, Bilbo stumbles along the dark tunnel.

Eventually, he comes across a subterranean lake, where Gollum dwells, a living vestige of a hobbit, his life preserved over centuries by the ring he has now lost for the first time. After a battle of riddles, Bilbo escapes, seemingly by luck, by slipping on the ring. Following the vengeful Gollum, who cannot see him, he finds his way out of the mountains, on the other side.

After the encounter with Gollum, the plucky Bilbo eventually leads the party successfully to the dragon's treasure, and the scaly monster perishes while attacking nearby Lake-town. Bilbo and Gandalf in the end journey back to the peaceful Shire—they have gone "there and back again." Bilbo decides to refuse most of his share of the treasure, having seen the results of greed. The events have in fact changed him forever, but even more, the ring he secretly possesses will shape the events eventually to be recorded in *The Lord of the Rings*.

TOM SHIPPEY ON SOURCES, ORIGINS, AND MODERNIZING THE PAST

The next point is that Tolkien did admit one possible source in Sinclair Lewis's novel *Babbitt* (1922), the story of the near-disgrace and abortive self-discovery of a complacent American businessman; to this theme the journey and the nature of Bilbo Baggins show some correspondence. But the source that Tolkien emphatically rejected is the word 'rabbit', of which so many critics have been reminded. 'Calling Bilbo a "nassty little rabbit" was a piece of vulgar trollery', he wrote, 'just as "descendant of rats" was a piece of dwarfish [sic] malice' (*Observer*, 20 February 1938). 'Certainly not rabbit,' he affirmed later. Internal evidence runs against him here, however, for it is not only the trolls who think simultaneously of Bilbo and rabbits. Bilbo makes the comparison himself in chapter 6 of *The Hobbit*, when he sees the eagle sharpening its beak and begins 'to think of being torn up for supper like a rabbit'. Three pages later the same thought occurs to the eagle: 'You need not be frightened like a rabbit, even if you look rather like one.' Thorin shakes Bilbo 'like a rabbit' in chapter 16, and much earlier Beorn—admittedly a rude and insensitive character—pokes Mr Baggins in the waist-coat and observes 'little bunny is getting nice and fat again' (p. 144). He is in a sense repaying the insult Bilbo offered earlier (p. 127), when he thought Beorn's 'skin-changing' meant he was 'a furrier, a man that calls rabbits conies, when he doesn't turn their skins into squirrels'. But the multiplicity of names gives a further clue to Tolkien's real thoughts, incubating since 1915 and the neologism 'coney-rabbits' in 'Goblin Feet'.

The fact is that 'rabbit' is a peculiar word. The *OED* can find no ultimate etymology for it, nor trace it back in English before 1398. 'Coney' or 'cunny' is little better, going back to 1302, while 'bunny' is a pet-name used originally for squirrels, as it happens, and not recorded till the seventeenth century. The words for 'rabbit' differ in several European languages (French *lapin*, German *kaninchen*), and there is no Old English or Old Norse word for it at all. These facts are unusual: 'hare', for instance, is paralleled by Old English *hara*, German *hase*, Old Norse *heri*, and so on, while the same could be said for 'weasel' or 'otter' or 'mouse' or 'brock' or most other familiar mammals of Northern Europe. The reason, of course, is that rabbits are immigrants. They appeared in England only round the thirteenth century, as imported creatures bred for fur, but escaped to the wild like mink or coypu. *Yet they have been assimilated.* The point is this: not one person in a thousand realises that rabbits (no Old English source) are in any historical way distinct from mice (O.E. *mýs*) or weasels (O.E. *weselas*), while the word is accepted by all as familiar, native, English. The creature has further established itself irreversibly in the folk-imagination, along with wise owls (O.E. *úlan*) and sly foxes (O.E. *fuhsas*). But if an Anglo-Saxon or Norseman had seen one he would have thought it alien, if not bizarre. Rabbits prove that novelties can be introduced into a language and then *made to fit*—of course as long as one exhibits due regard to deep structures of language and thought. 'If a foreign word falls by chance into the stream of a language', wrote Jacob Grimm, 'it is rolled around till it takes on that language's colour, and in spite of its foreign nature comes to look like a native one.'

Now this situation of anachronism-cum-familiarity certainly has *something* to do with hobbits. The first time that Bilbo Baggins appears in close focus he is 'standing at his door after breakfast smoking an enormous long wooden pipe'. Smoking later appears as not just a characteristic of hobbits, but virtually *the* characteristic, 'the one art that we can certainly claim to be our own invention', declares Meriadoc Brandybuck (*LOTR*, p. 8). But what are they smoking besides pipes? '*Pipeweed*, or *leaf*', declares the *Lord of the Rings* Prologue firmly. Why not say 'tobacco', since the plant is 'a variety probably of *Nicotiana*'? Because the word would sound wrong. It is an import from some unknown Caribbean language via Spanish, reaching English only after the discovery of America, sometime in the sixteenth century. The words it resembles most are 'potato' and 'tomato', also referring to new objects from America, eagerly adopted in England and naturalised with great speed, but marked off as foreign by their very phonetic structure. 'Pipeweed' shows Tolkien's wish to accept a common feature of English modernity, which he knew could not exist in the ancient world of elves or trolls, and whose anachronism would instantly be betrayed by a word with the foreign feel of 'tobacco'. Actually Bilbo *does* use 'tobacco' on page 14 of *The Hobbit*, and Gandalf mentions 'tomatoes' not much later. *In the first edition*. The third changes 'cold chicken and tomatoes' to 'cold chicken and pickles'," and after that the foreign fruit is excluded. 'Potatoes' stay in, being indeed the speciality of Gaffer Gamgee, but his son Sam has a habit of assimilating the word to the more native-sounding 'taters'—Tolkien notes elsewhere that the word was borrowed into colloquial Welsh from colloquial English as *tatws*, in which form it sounds much less distinctive ('EW', p. 34). But in fact the scene in which Sam discusses 'taters' with Gollum (*LOTR*, p. 640) is a little cluster of anachronisms: hobbits, eating rabbits (Sam calls them 'coveys'), wishing for potatoes ('taters') but out of tobacco ('pipeweed'). One day, offers Sam to Gollum, he might cook him something better—'fried fish and chips'. Nothing could now be more distinctively English! Not much would be *less* distinctively Old English. The hobbits, though, are on our side of many cultural boundaries.

That, then, is their association with rabbits. One can see why Tolkien denied the obvious connection between the two: he did not want hobbits classified as small, furry creatures, vaguely 'cute' just as fairies were vaguely 'pretty'. On the other hand both insinuated themselves, rabbits into the homely company of fox and goose and hen, hobbits into the fantastic but equally verbally authenticated set of elves and dwarves and orcs and ettens. One might go so far as to say that the absence of rabbits from ancient legend made them not an 'asterisk word' but an 'asterisk thing'—maybe they were there but nobody noticed. That is exactly the ecological niche Tolkien selected for hobbits, 'an *unobtrusive* but *very ancient* people' (*LOTR*, p. 1, my italics). It is not likely that this role was devised for them before the arrival of the inspired 'In a hole in the ground there lived a hobbit', any more than the etymology from *holbytla*. Still, the amazing thing about that sentence, looking back, is the readiness with which it responded to development. The first half of it helped to anchor hobbits in history, via *holbytlan*, the second to characterise them in fiction, via the anachronisms associated with the rabbit-analogy. Such complexity could be the result of prior unconscious cogitation or later artistic effort. Either way, 'hobbit' as word and concept threw out its anchors into Old and modern English at once: 'grammarye' at work once more.

Breaking Contact

This preamble makes it easier to say what Tolkien was doing in *The Hobbit*. Like Walter Scott or William Morris before him, he felt the perilous charm of the archaic world of the North, recovered from bits and scraps by generations of inquiry. He wanted to tell a story about it simply, one feels, because there were hardly any complete ones left; *Beowulf* or *The Saga of King Heidrek* stimulated the imagination but did not satisfy it. Accordingly he created a sort of 'asterisk-world' for the Norse *Elder Edda*. The dwarf-names of 'Thorin and Company', as well as Gandalf's, come from a section of the Eddic poem *Völuspá*, often known as the *Dvergatal* or 'Dwarves' Roster'. This is not much regarded now, and has been called a 'rigma-role', a meaningless list; *The Hobbit* implies, though, that that meaningless list is the last faded memento of something once great and important, an Odyssey of the dwarves. As for the landscape through which Gandalf, Thorin and the rest move, that too is an Eddic one; 'the pathless Mirkwood' is mentioned in several poems, while 'the Misty Mountains' come from the poem *Skirnismál*, where Freyr's page, sent to abduct the giant's daughter, says grimly to his horse:

> 'Myrct er úti, mál gveð ec ocr fara
>   úrig fiöll yfir
>   Þyrsa pbióð yfir;
> báðir við komomc, eða ocr báða tecr
>   sá inn ámátki iotunn.

> 'The mirk is outside, I call it our business to fare over the misty mountains, over the tribes of orcs (*Þyrs* = *orc*; . . .); we will both come back, or else he will take us both, he the mighty giant.'

All that Tolkien has done, in a way, is to make place-names out of adjectives, to turn words into things.

But there is one very evident obstacle to recreating the ancient world of heroic legend for modern readers, and that lies in the nature of heroes. These are not acceptable anymore, and tend very strongly to be treated with irony: the modern view of *Beowulf* is John Gardner's novel *Grendel* (1971). Tolkien did not want to be ironic about heroes, and yet he could not eliminate modern reactions. His response to the difficulty is Bilbo Baggins, the hobbit, the anachronism, a character whose initial role at least is very strongly that of mediator. He represents and often voices modern opinions, modern incapacities: he has no impulses towards revenge or self-conscious heroism, cannot 'hoot twice like a barn-owl and once like a screech owl' as the dwarves suggest, knows almost nothing about Wilderland, and cannot even skin a rabbit, being used to having his meat 'delivered by the butcher all ready to cook'. Yet he has a place in the ancient world too, and there is a hint that (just like us) all his efforts cannot keep him entirely separate from the past.

It seems that, in spite of the illusion of progress, human beings have undergone little inward change. Because of this, present-day readers are still fascinated by the stories and narrative motifs that our ancestors created and dispersed. So, the success of books such as *Harry Potter*, Philip Pullman's trilogy *His Dark Materials*, and also J.R.R. Tolkien's fantasy of Middle-earth, which captivate the imagination of children and teenagers, owes much to the motifs and elements that have characterized literature across the ages.

The Hobbit is a story Tolkien wrote to tell to his sons at night. When he began writing *The Lord of the Rings*, his sons were grown up and did no longer want bedtime stories. We agree with Humphrey Carpenter (1977: 200) on the idea that *The Hobbit* is a children's story, although it has been integrated into a mythology intended for a more adult reader and was written in a more serious tone. The author's original idea when writing the story of Bilbo was for it to be entertaining and amusing for his first audience, his sons. This work does not aspire to achieve the emotional and moral intensity of *The Lord of the Rings*. The title of the book *The Hobbit*, or, *There and Back Again* declares an uninhibited narrative tone. The literary style is indeed very relaxed and the work has a great structural simplicity. Only in the battle of the Five Armies episode do the details of the troops' movement take on the sophistication of modern warfare and the devotion of the participants reaches an epic height. Tolkien's short fiction has maintained the light style characteristic of *The Hobbit*.

The narrator of Bilbo's story is omniscient, frequently discusses the events described and constantly speaks to the reader as if to a child. As early as the first paragraphs we read: "He may have lost the neighbours' respect, but he gained—well, you will see whether he gained anything in the end" (H, 16).[1] The narrator's knowledge about the elements of the story is superior to that of the characters. In this way, when Bilbo finds the Ring, the narrator comments: "It was a turning point in his career, but he did not know it" (H, 76). Or we can also read "Now, if you wish, like the dwarves, to hear news of Smaug, you must go back again to the evening when he smashed the door and flew off in rage, two days before" (H, 234). The narrator is aware of the reader's cognitive universe. Therefore, he can predict the reader's reactions: "The mother of our particular Hobbit—what is a Hobbit? I suppose Hobbits need some description nowadays" (H, 16). When he thinks there is enough information to follow the recounted events, he abandons description of the hobbits: "Now you know enough to go on with" (H, 16). Sometimes he deliberately conceals pieces of information in order to generate interest: "Gandalf! If you had heard only a quarter of what I have heard about him, and I have only heard very little of all there is to hear, you would be prepared for any sort of remarkable tale" (H, 17). On other occasions, he omits data that the reader already knows: "You are familiar with Thorin's style on important occasions, so I will not give you any more of it, though he went on a good deal longer than this" (H, 203). The narrator also establishes a direct dialogue with the reader; because of this, he is sometimes mentioned: "There is little or no magic about them, except the ordinary everyday sort which helps them to disappear quietly and quickly when large stupid folk like you and me come blundering along" (H, 16); or also in "There was a lot here which Smaug did not understand at all (though I expect you do, since you know all about Bilbo's adventures to which he was referring)" (H, 213). He also addresses the reader with a direct, conversational tone: "As I was saying, the mother of this Hobbit" (H, 16) or "whether you believe it or not" (H, 273). Moreover, he is conscious of the fact that his narration is in a written medium, as the narrator explains, referring to a song by the dwarves: "Then off they went into another song as ridiculous as the one I have written in full" (H, 59). On another occasion, he postpones reporting the adventure: "[H]e began to wonder what had become of his unfortunate friends. It was not very long before he discovered; but that belongs to the next chapter" (H, 166). We can notice the childlike tone of certain expressions: "(If you want to know what *cram* is, I can only say that I don't know the recipe; but it is biscuitish, keeps good indefinitely, is supposed to be sustaining, and is certainly not entertaining, being in fact very uninteresting except as a chewing exercise. It was made by the Lake-men for long journeys" (H, 232).

The Hobbit is a well-established book in the tradition of children's narrative, of which the most notable exponents in British letters are Lewis Carroll, Kenneth Grahame, Beatrix Potter and George Macdonald. As Lois R. Kuznets (1981: 150–151) has shown, Bilbo's story fits into the rhetorical structure of children's fiction, which combines the following features: an omniscient narrator that comments on events and addresses the reader directly, characters preadolescent children can easily identify with, an emphasis on the relationship between time and narrative development within the framework of a condensed narrative time, and a defined geography in which safe and dangerous spaces are separate. These characteristics are evident to a greater degree in Bilbo's story than in Frodo's. Two features mark the difference between the tones of these novels. As far as the relation between time and narrative development is concerned, the action in *The Hobbit* covers approximately one year and emphasizes the changes in season. The characters' movements in space correspond to the seasonal changes.

Bilbo fits into the rhetoric of children's fantasy more than Frodo does because the former is a character that does not evolve at all throughout the story, and the events in which he takes part seem not to affect him. The hobbits and the dwarves, because of their height, their cheerful personalities and their habits are creatures with which a young reader can easily identify. The hobbit houses, holes hidden in the mountainside, speak very well to the child's inclination to hide in small places. Just like children, hobbits are fond of riddles, puns and lexical creativity that sometimes transgress grammatical norms. They are also curious to hear old tales and stories. Their habits of eating six times a day, of going barefoot, etc. bring them closer to childlike behaviour. The songs the main characters sing in *The Hobbit* are to a large extent cheerful, insubstantial and suitable for the enjoyment of little ones. In general, these songs intensify the lively tone of the story and show the joyous personalities of the singers, usually hobbits and dwarves. However, the aim of the songs and poems inserted in passages of great dramatic or emotional tension in *The Lord of the Rings* is to introduce a peaceful moment and to create an aesthetic distance. As in the epic poems sung in the Middle Ages, those who recite the poems and elegiac songs in *The Lord of the Rings* are creators of honour. In these works, life and literature merge.

Note

1. The title of Tolkien's works will be abbreviated as follows: *The Hobbit* (H), *The Fellowship of the Ring* (I), *The Two Towers* (II), *The Return of the King* (III), and *The Silmarillion* (S).

Works Cited

Carpenter, H., ed., and C. Tolkien, assistant. 1981. *The Letters of J. R. R. Tolkien*. London: HarperCollins.

Carpenter, H. 1977. *The Inklings. C. S. Lewis, J. R. R. Tolkien, Charles Williams*. London: George Allen & Unwin.

Colomer, T. 1998. *La formació del lector literari*. Barcelona: Barcanova.

Grotta, D. 1976. *The Biography of J. R. R. Tolkien*. Philadelphia, Pennsylvania: Running Press.

Kuznets, L. R. 1981. "Tolkien and the Rhetoric of Childhood". *Tolkien. New Critical Perspectives*. Ed. N. D. Isaacs et al. Lexington, Kentucky: The University Press of Kentucky. 150–162.

Shippey, T. A. 1992. *The Road to Middle Earth*. London: HarperCollins Publishers.

Tolkien, C., ed. 2002. *The History of Middle-earth*. Thirteen volumes. New York: Ballantine Books.

Tolkien, J. R. R. 1969 (1954). *The Two Towers*. New York: Ballantine Books.

———. 1973 (1937). *The Hobbit*. New York: Ballantine.

———. 1973 (1954). *The Return of the King*. New York: Ballantine.

———. 1979 (1954). *The Fellowship of the Ring*. New York: Ballantine.

———. 1979 (1977). *The Silmarillion*. Ed. C. Tolkien. New York: Ballantine.

———. 1997 (1947). "On Fairy Stories". *The Monsters and the Critics and Other Essays*. Ed. C. Tolkien. London: HarperCollins. 109–161.

West, R. C. 1975. "The Interlace Structure of *The Lord of the Rings*". *A Tolkien Compass*. Ed. J. Lobdell. New York: Ballantine. 82–102.

Many of the important swords in *The Hobbit* and *The Lord of
the Rings* are inscribed with runes. As Tolkien himself explains
in *The Hobbit*, "Runes were old letters originally used for cutting or scratching on wood, stone, or metal, and so were thin
and angular" (note preceding ch. 1). Tolkien says that the use
of runes in Middle-earth at the time of *The Hobbit* was largely
limited to the dwarves (although Gandalf later leaves a runic
inscription at Weathertop for Strider [I.xi.198–9]); both the
Anglo-Saxons and the Scandinavians, however, made extensive use of them (Page; Elliott), providing a nice link between
Tolkien's imaginary world and the real world that occupied his
scholarly life.[6] When Glamdring, Orcrist, and Sting are first
found in the cave of the trolls in *The Hobbit*, Gandalf remarks
that "These look like good blades [. . .]. They were not made
by any troll, nor by any smith among men in these parts and
days; but when we can read the runes on them, we shall know
more about them" (2.51). The nature of the blades is made
clearer when the party arrives at Rivendell, and Elrond, who
"knew all about runes of every kind," examines the swords:

> "They are old swords, very old swords of the High Elves
> of the West, my kin. They were made in Gondolin for
> the Goblin-wars. They must have come from a dragon's
> hoard or goblin plunder, for dragons and goblins
> destroyed that city many ages ago. This, Thorin, the
> runes name Orcrist, the Goblin-cleaver in the ancient
> tongue of Gondolin; it was a famous blade. This, Gandalf,
> was Glamdring, Foe-hammer that the king of Gondolin
> once wore. Keep them well!" (3.59)

. . . As swords with runic inscriptions, the Middle-earth blades
may be placed in a rich tradition of medieval sword-lore. Tolkien's 1936 lecture on *Beowulf* changed the face of *Beowulf* scholarship, and Beowulf's battle with Grendel's dam is dominated

by swords.[8] The first is Hrunting, loaned to Beowulf by Unferð and said to be damascened and ring-patterned on its edge (1459 and 1521).[9] The giant-sword taken by Beowulf from the monsters' lair beneath the lake is likewise "ring-marked" and inscribed with a wavy pattern (1564 and 1616), as is Beowulf's (un-named) sword at 1489. Although the blade of the giant-sword melts "just like ice" (1608), Beowulf returns to Heorot and presents the hilt to Hrothgar:

> Hrothgar spoke—he studied the hilt
> of the old heirloom, where was written the origin
> of ancient strife [. . .].
> . . . .
> Also, on the sword-guard of bright gold
> was rightly marked in rune-letters,
> set down and said for whom that sword,
> best of irons, had first been made,
> with scrollery and serpentine patterns. (1687–89, 1694–98)

Another Anglo-Saxon poem, *Solomon and Saturn* (identified by Shippey, *Author* 24–5 as a source for some of Gollum's riddles in the riddle-game in *The Hobbit*, chapter 5), contains one of the few identified references in literature to the cutting of runes upon a sword, where it is said of the Devil that "He writes upon his weapon a great number of deathmarks, baleful letters; he cuts them on his sword" (qtd. in Davidson, *Sword* 151).[10] Similarly, in the *Saga of the Volsungs* (a work which Tolkien knew well),[11] the Valkyrie Brynhild gives Sigurd knowledge of "victory runes" which are carved in the hilt and blade of a sword:

> Victory runes shall you know
> If you want to secure wisdom,
> And cut them on the sword hilt,
> On the center ridge of the blade,
> And the parts of the brand,
> And name Tyr twice. (ch. 21, p. 68)

. . . Just as many of the swords of Middle-earth carry runes and ornamentation, so too can most be considered ancient heirlooms. Thus, as we have seen, Elrond remarks of Orcrist and Glamdring that they "are old swords, very old" (3.59). Just how formidable a reputation Orcrist enjoyed is further revealed when the sword is discovered in the possession of Thorin by the Goblins under the Misty Mountains:

> The Great Goblin gave a truly awful howl of rage when he looked at it, and all his soldiers gnashed their teeth, clashed their shields, and stamped. They knew the sword at once. It had killed hundreds of goblins in its time, when the fair elves of Gondolin hunted them in the hills or did battle before their walls. They had called it Orcrist, Goblin-cleaver, but the goblins called it simply Biter. They hated it and hated worse any one that carried it. (4.70)

More obvious in this regard, however, is Narsil, the Sword that was Broken, the shards of which have been passed down from generation to generation within the kindred of Elendil. Thus Aragorn proclaims at the Council of Elrond: "For the Sword that was Broken [. . .] has been treasured by his heirs when all other heirlooms were lost" (II.ii.260; cf. App. A, §I(iii) 323). The sword's importance is further attested when Aragorn, forced to leave Anduril outside the gates of Meduseld, threatens reprisals to any who should touch it (III.vi.115); the passing reference here to the sword's being forged by Telchar is part of its mystique.[16] Mention should be made in this context of another important weapon—not a sword this time—that is handed down from generation to generation in Middle-earth: the arrow that Bard uses to slay Smaug (*Hobbit* 14.236). As Shippey remarks, the arrow denotes Bard's heroic heritage as well as some of the more epic-heroic aspects of *The Hobbit* (*Author* 39).

Notes
6. In this sense we have a variant of Tolkien's use of philology to recreate or create a past world or mythology. On Tolkien's use of philology see Shippey, *Road* passim.

8. Unless otherwise stated, all references to *Beowulf* are by line number to the Liuzza translation. Quotations in Anglo-Saxon are from the Klaeber edition.

9. Although *atertanum fah* (1459) literally means "[decorated or] etched with poison-stripes" (as Liuzza translates), it probably reflects ornamental markings and so could be translated as "adorned with deadly crawling patternings." See Wrenn and Bolton, ed., *Beowulf* n. to 1459, and Klaeber, ed., *Beowulf* n. to 1459b–60a. Liuzza's "ornamented" for *brodenmael* (1616) might also be more specific (if less elegant), something like "damascened" or "woven with a wavy pattern."

10. We wonder if there is an echo here of the inscription engraved by Sauron on the One Ring.

11. Tolkien had composed a long, unpublished poem in Old Norse based upon the Edda material dealing with Sigurd and Gunnar: see *Letters* pp. 379 and 452.

16. Telchar's identity is alluded to but not explained; he seems to be a sort of primeval master craftsman, not unlike Wayland the Smith in Germanic myth or Ilmarinen the "everlasting craftsman" who forged the sky and the mysterious Sampo in the Finnish *Kalevala* 10: 277–8, 281ff. Elsewhere Telchar is identified as a dwarf smith, but it seems reasonable to suppose that Tolkien had these archetypes in mind—the *Kalevala* is certainly known to have been of considerable interest to him.

Elizabeth A. Whittingham on the Influence of Family on Tolkien

The final, but not least important, of the significant events and major influences in Tolkien's life was his family. During Tolkien's professional years when his relationships with the Inklings, Lewis, and other scholars and writers developed, Tolkien also coexisted in another world, that of his wife and children. Pearce believes that the attention writers have paid to Tolkien's male friends, both those of his youth and those of his adult life, has overshadowed his family's importance to him. In response to Charles Moseley's assertion that Tolkien was most affected by his beliefs, his "experience of" World War I, and "the nature of Oxford academic life and society" (qtd. in Pearce 40), Pearce writes, "Without denigrating any of these, all of which influenced his work to a greater or lesser degree, [Tolkien's] role as storyteller and *paterfamilias* to his children was equally important, at least initially" (40). In particular, he identifies the four Tolkien children—John, Michael, Christopher, and Priscilla—as providing the impetus for their father's storytelling: "Indeed, it is fair to assume that if Tolkien had remained a bachelor and had not been blessed with children he would never have written either *The Hobbit* or *The Lord of the Rings*. Perhaps he would have written The Silmarillion, but in all probability it would never have been published" (40). The role of the family as an influence on Tolkien's work is an ongoing theme throughout Pearce's biography and reflects the Catholic values that Tolkien held.

Many of Tolkien's letters support Pearce's assertions, especially as concerns the author's consideration of his children as the audience for his writings. In a 1964 letter, he describes his creation of "stories" to entertain them and explains that he originally had meant *The Hobbit* as such a tale (*Letters* 346). Earlier, in 1959, he had provided a similar account, commenting that he presupposed that "children and fairy-stories" possessed a unique bond (298). Tolkien often commented on the fact that he repented of the style in which he had written *The Hobbit*. In a 1955 letter to Auden, he apologizes for its "silliness of manner" and observes that his own offspring had been too young to put him right concerning his misassumption (215). Tolkien's comments support Pearce's argument that in the beginning the author's family, especially his four children, were his audience and impacted the type of stories he wrote.

Many authors have written about Tolkien's relationship with his wife, Edith, and have speculated about the couple's relationship. An early point of contention was Tolkien's insistence that Edith become a Roman Catholic soon after their engagement, and differences in their beliefs seem to have caused some discord throughout their marriage. Pearce discusses certain of their arguments in detail and strongly criticizes John Carey, whose review of Carpenter's biography jumps to some unwarranted conclusions (qtd. in Pearce 46). Pearce praises Brian Rosebury's reasonable response to

Carey's assertion that Tolkien required his wife to confess to a priest when they engaged in marital relations and that her vehement resistance to such requests was a source of contention between them (47). Rosebury points out that Carpenter's biography does not corroborate Carey's assertions, and that "here it is Carey, not Tolkien, who takes it for granted that the mere practice of sexual intercourse may be a Catholic's motive for confession" (158). Additionally, none of Tolkien's writings—and he does discuss sexual intercourse in his letters—supports any such idea. Most of the biographies assert that Edith was uneasy with certain aspects of Catholicism, thought her husband spent too much time away from home, and felt isolated in Oxford and uncomfortable with her husband's academic friends—Lewis in particular.

Not surprisingly, the letters that the family shared with Carpenter for publication reveal—for the most part—little of consequence about the marriage itself. The facts are that they lived together for fifty-five years, raised four children, and took family vacations. Edith followed her husband where he went, though there are indications that she was unhappy with the move from Leeds to Oxford, and in retirement Tolkien followed his wife to Bournemouth, though he returned to Oxford shortly after her death. The letters indicate that they nursed each other through various ailments, and the History of Middle-earth provides evidence that now and then Edith helped her husband by making fair copies of some of his manuscripts. Edith, according to her husband, took care of household matters, and on occasion, they went out to dinner together and entertained friends and acquaintances in their home. The bare facts are few and unrevealing.

No one can know what goes on between a married couple in the privacy of their home—even children are neither impartial nor fully informed observers—and long-term relationships are a complex matter. In one often-quoted letter to Christopher, Tolkien reflects on the sixty-three years the couple had known one another. The context, however, is important: Tolkien is writing to his son less than a year after his wife's death, informing him of the decision he has made about the inscription for her tombstone. He prefaces his comments by noting the improbability of his ever producing an autobiography and explaining that he thinks "someone," apparently Christopher, ought to be informed about certain facts (*Letters* 421). Tolkien refers to his and Edith's difficult "childhoods" and the pain that they had each gone through, which might help in understanding some of the tough times they had experienced, but he avows that their "youthful love" was great and always strong (421). The portrayal, though including elements of both light and dark, seems dismal and painful, but is likely colored by the loss of his life's companion and by introspection growing out of his contemplation of his own mortality. Certainly, these lines to his son emphasize the complexity inherent within any relationship and the futility of an outsider attempting to say much that is of significance. Whatever their relationship, Tolkien often attributed to Edith the role of inspiration for certain images and stories.

The family member, however, who stands out as making the most crucial contribution to the author's work is his son, Christopher. The youngest of the author's three sons, Christopher assisted his father in many ways: reading and commenting on versions of the story, drawing maps, and after his father's death, editing and publishing volumes of the author's manuscripts. Though Tolkien and Christopher's separation because of World War II was difficult for them, scholars and fans benefited from their being apart during the years that *The Lord of the Rings* was being written. Because of their distance and the lengthy letters from father to son, readers have had a window into Tolkien's mind and the creative process involved in his writing of this important work. That Tolkien valued his son's input and help is clear in many letters. Having sent to Christopher the latest two chapters of *The Lord of the Rings*, the father asks in one 1944 letter for his son's feedback, stating, "for a long time now I have written with you most in mind" (*Letters* 103). In a letter to publisher Stanley Unwin a few months later, Tolkien describes his son's role in more detail, depicting him as his most important reader, one who checked the text, typed it, and drew the "maps" (112–13). This description and other similar ones indicate that Tolkien relied on and valued his son's feedback and help.

The letters that Tolkien wrote during World War II to Christopher and to his second oldest son, Michael, reveal not only how much they meant to him but also something about their father–son relationships and about Tolkien's personal faith. Not surprisingly, one thought on his mind was that he might not see his sons again, and he refers to that fear in letters to each of them. Tolkien encourages Michael and reminds him that they are connected spiritually, upholding their hope of "heaven" (*Letters* 55). In one wartime letter, Tolkien commends Christopher to his "guardian angel" (66), and in another, writing of their love for one another, declares his belief in eternity and his confidence that their "special bond" will survive death (76). He encourages his sons to attend mass when they can and to sing songs of praise to God when they cannot. Tolkien writes of his own faith openly and naturally, suggesting that he has often spoken of spiritual matters to his sons. To Christopher, he describes a "vision" that came to him in church that he believed to be the presence of God (*Letters* 99). Later in the same letter, Tolkien mentions going to mass with his daughter, Priscilla, on another day, telling about the sermon, his own response, and his gratification in seeing a devout "old man" who had also worshipped at St. Gregory's (101). He situates such stories between his chronicle of daily events and the latest chapter of *The Lord of the Rings*. Consequently, his spiritual life and the practice of his faith seem as natural and as normal as eating a meal, bicycling to town, or cleaning the hen house.

Tolkien's letters to his children, both during wartime and throughout their lives, are frank and honest. Though he offers advice on everything from sex to religion and from dealing with the oppression of war to surviving college politics, he also shares his own fears and acknowledges his own failures. He confesses to Michael that from 1920 to 1930 that he provided a poor example since he did not attend mass as regularly as he should have. Describing his inability to escape the faith of his youth, he expresses his remorse and "regret," revealing the "silent appeal of Tabernacle, and . . . starving hunger" that always draws him back (*Letters* 340). Because of the strength and enduring nature of his faith, Tolkien can admit not only his failures but also his doubts; however, he affirms that his faith is stronger than passing feelings or temporary lapses. To his family, Tolkien does not offer pretense but honesty, writing about his personal beliefs with sincerity and candor. He holds both his family and his faith as essential elements of his life, and both clearly affected who he was as a man and an author.

Works by J.R.R. Tolkien

Edited by Tolkien

Sir Gawain and the Green Knight, 1925

Ancrene Wissee: The English Text of Ancrene Riwle, 1962

Major Publications

A Middle English Vocabulary, 1922

The Hobbit, or There and Back Again, 1937

Farmer Giles of Ham, 1950

The Fellowship of the Ring, 1954

The Two Towers, 1954

The Return of the King, 1955

The Adventures of Tom Bombadil and Other Verses from the Red Book, 1962

Tree and Leaf, 1964

The Tolkien Reader, 1966

The Road Goes Ever On: A Song Cycle, 1967

Smith of Wootton Major, 1967

Posthumous Publications

Sir Gawain and the Green Knight, Pearl, and Sir Orfeo, 1975

The Father Christmas Letters, 1976

The Simarillion, 1977

Pictures by J.R.R. Tolkien, 1979

Unfinished Tales of Numenor and Middle Earth, 1980

Old English Exodus, 1981

Finn and Hengest: The Fragment and the Episode 1982

Mr. Bliss, 1983

The Monsters and the Critics and Other Essays. 1983

Beowulf and the Critics, 2002

Annotated Bibliography

Birzer, Bradley. *J.R.R. Tolkien's Sanctifying Myth: Understanding Middle Earth*. Wilmington, DE: Isi Books, 2002.

This in-depth study of the religious themes and symbols in Tolkien's body of work situates the author within the Christian humanist tradition.

Bloom, Harold. *J.R.R. Tolkien*. Modern Critical Views. New York: Chelsea House Publishers, 2008.

This anthology-style volume provides several essays by prominent Tolkien critics. The essays cover a range of Tolkien's writing and provide a good overview of his critical reception.

Bramlett, Perry C. *I Am in Fact a Hobbit: An Introduction to the Life and Work of J.R.R. Tolkien*. Macon, GA: Mercer University Press, 2003.

This general study of Tolkien's life and writings include his lesser-known and unpublished works. Aimed at a general readership, this would be a good text for precollege students to consult.

Carpenter, Humphrey. *J.R.R. Tolkien: A Biography*. Boston: Houghton Mifflin, 1987.

Generally regarded as the authoritative Tolkien biography, the text covers Tolkien's life from his birth in South Africa to his death in England. It deftly combines historical information about the author with critical information about his writing.

Crabbe, Katharyn W. *J.R.R. Tolkien*. New York: Continuum Press, 1988.

A comprehensive study of Tolkien's life and writing, the critical study is organized around the quest motif. Chapter two, "The Quest as Fairy Tale: *The Hobbit*," provides a genre study of the novel.

Croft, Janet Brennan, ed. *Tolkien and Shakespeare: Shared Themes and Language*. Jefferson, NC: McFarland, 2007.

The essays in this collection explore some of the themes, ideas, and character types the two authors shared in exploring the influence of Shakespeare on Tolkien's creative process. It is especially useful for exploring the presentation of "faerie" elements in each of the writer's works.

Dickerson, Matthew, and Jonathan Evans. *Ents, Elves and Eriador: The Environmental Vision of J.R.R. Tolkien*. Lexington: University of Kentucky Press, 2006.

A comprehensive and in-depth study of Tolkien's environmental vision and the role it played in shaping his mythology and writing, this is an indispensable text for anyone exploring the role of nature or the environment in Tolkien's body of work.

Duriez, Colin. *Tolkien and C.S. Lewis: The Gift of Friendship*. Mahwah, NJ: Hidden Spring Press, 2003.

A study of the friendship between Tolkien and Lewis and the impact and influence each had on the other's writing. Chapter six deals specifically with the writing of *The Hobbit*.

Fimi, Dimitra. *Tolkien, Race, and Cultural History: From Fairies to Hobbits*. London: Palgrave Macmillan, 2009.

Fimi uses a historical perspective to examine Tolkien's writings, providing a cultural history of the Victorian and Edwardian periods. The author examines discourses of race and masculinity in Tolkien's time, arguing that Tolkien's ideas developed out of his interaction with contemporary thinking.

Flieger, Verlyn. *Logos and Language in Tolkien's World*. Kent, OH: Kent State University Press, 2002.

This study applies Owen Barfield's linguistic theory of the fragmentation of meaning to Tolkien's body of work. The study connects Tolkien's symbolism, especially light symbolism, to the culture and language of Middle-Earth.

———. *A Question of Time: J.R.R. Tolkien's Road to Faerie*. Kent, OH: Kent State University Press, 1997.

Flieger's access to Tolkien's manuscripts and unpublished writing allowed him to present several new ideas about the origin and gestation of Tolkien's texts and the critical responses to them. Flieger uses Tolkien's presentation of time to help construct the author's mythology and notes how his mythology exists in a "troubled and critical" relationship with Tolkien's historical period.

Garth, John. *Tolkien and the Great War: The Threshold of Middle Earth*. Boston: Houghton Mifflin, 2003.

Offering an in-depth study of Tolkein and his circle at the time of World War I, the text is notable for its detailed study of the war experience and record of Tolkien and his college friends, connecting Tolkien's time in the war and a military hospital with the beginning of his writing career.

Grotta, Daniel. *J.R.R. Tolkien: Architect of Middle Earth*. Philadelphia: Running Press, 1992.

Grotta's general biography is a good introduction for the general reader to the author's life and works.

Hume, Kathryn. *Fantasy and Mimesis*: *Responses to Reality in Western Literature*. New York: Methuen, 1984.

Hume's study focuses on the literary motives for an author's departure from conventions of reality. The author also explores the techniques writers use to produce such effects, finding Bilbo Baggins a "low mimetic hero."

O'Neil, Timothy. *The Individuated Hobbit: Jung, Tolkien, and the Arch-Types of Middle Earth*. Boston: Houghton Mifflin, 1979.

In its Jungian analysis of Tolkien's fiction, this companion work offers an insightful chapter providing analysis of Bilbo.

Petty, Anne. *Tolkien in the Land of Heroes*. Cold Spring Harbor, NY: Cold Spring Press 2003.

This volume presents a comprehensive study of the themes and the internal mythology of Tolkien's major fiction.

Rateliff, John D. *The History of the Hobbit: Part One—Mr. Baggins* and *The History of the Hobbit: Part Two—Return to Bag-End.* Boston: Houghton Mifflin, 2007.

This multivolume set offers the best textual history of *The Hobbit* to date. The study presents the manuscript of *The Hobbit* with analysis, commentary, and source scholarship. It also presents the official revisions Tolkien made to the manuscript, as well as an account of Tolkien's thoughts about possibly rewriting the entire book.

Rosebury, Brian. *Tolkien: A Cultural Phenomenon.* New York: Palgrave MacMillian, 2003.

A good defense of the critical and artistic merit of Tolkien and of Tolkien studies, Rosebury's volume concludes that *The Hobbit* is "a likeable patchwork of accomplishments, blunders, and tantalizing promises of Middle Earth yet to come." The author sees the novel as flawed by inconsistencies of tone and conception, viewing it as a transitional work, a steppingstone in Tolkien's creative journey.

———. *Tolkien: A Critical Assessment.* New York: St. Martin's Press, 1992.

Rosebury sought to "arrive at a view of Tolkien which places him in the same frame as other twentieth-century writers, explores his originality and modernity" (6). The text is accessible and usefully organized, a good starting point for a research paper.

Shippey, Tom. *The Road to Middle Earth: How J.R.R. Tolkien Created a New Mythology.* Boston: Houghton Mifflin, 2003.

Tom Shippey is one of the most respected critics writing about Tolkien and his work. Generally considered Shippey's best work, this volume is required reading for any serious critical work on Tolkien or his books.

Tolkien Studies: An Annual Scholarly Review, edited by Douglas A. Anderson and Michael D.C. Drout. Morgantown: West Virginia University Press.

This journal presents the growing body of critical commentary and scholarship on the entire Tolkien canon.

Walker, Steve. *The Power of Tolkien's Prose: Middle Earth's Magical Style*. New York: Palgrave-Macmillan, 2009.

An in-depth and rewarding study of Tolkien's prose style, Walker's volume employs more of a close reading than a theoretical reflection of Tolkien's style. Although a scholarly text, Walker's study is accessible to the general reader and includes an extensive bibliography and notes.

Whittingham, Elizabeth. *The Evolution of Tolkien's Mythology: A Study of the History of Middle Earth*. Jefferson: McFarland and Company, 2008.

A valuable resource, Whittingham uses Christopher Tolkien's 12-volume *History of Middle Earth* to refashion our understanding of Tolkien's creative process and the growth and evolution of Tolkien's complex mythology.

Contributors

Harold Bloom is Sterling Professor of the Humanities at Yale University. Educated at Cornell and Yale universities, he is the author of more than 30 books, including *Shelley's Mythmaking* (1959), *Blake's Apocalypse* (1963), *Yeats* (1970), *The Anxiety of Influence* (1973), *A Map of Misreading* (1975), *Kabbalah and Criticism* (1975), *Agon: Toward a Theory of Revisionism* (1982), *The American Religion* (1992), *The Western Canon* (1994), *Omens of Millennium: The Gnosis of Angels, Dreams, and Resurrection* (1996), *Shakespeare: The Invention of the Human* (1998), *How to Read and Why* (2000), *Genius: A Mosaic of One Hundred Exemplary Creative Minds* (2002), *Hamlet: Poem Unlimited* (2003), *Where Shall Wisdom Be Found?* (2004), *Jesus and Yahweh: The Names Divine* (2005), and *Till I End My Song: A Gathering of Last Poems* (2010). In addition, he is the author of hundreds of articles, reviews, and editorial introductions. In 1999, Professor Bloom received the American Academy of Arts and Letters' Gold Medal for Criticism. He has also received the International Prize of Catalonia, the Alfonso Reyes Prize of Mexico, and the Hans Christian Andersen Bicentennial Prize of Denmark.

Katharyn W. Crabbe was associate professor of English at Sonoma State University. She is the author of *J.R.R. Tolkien* and *Evelyn Waugh*.

Brain Rosebury is principal lecturer in English in the department of the humanities, University of Central Lancashire in the United Kingdom. He is the author of *Tolkien: A Critical Assessment* and *Art and Desire: A Study in the Aesthetics of Fiction*.

Humphrey Carpenter is the author of *J.R.R. Tolkien: A Biography*, *W.H. Auden: A Biography*, *The Inklings*, and coeditor of *The Letters of J.R.R. Tolkien*.

Perry C. Bramlett is the author of *I Am in Fact a Hobbit: An Introduction to the Life and Work of J.R.R. Tolkien* and *A C.S. Lewis Spiritual Reader,* coauthor (with Ronald W. Higdon) of *C.S. Lewis: Life at the Center* and *Touring C.S. Lewis' Ireland and England,* and a contributor to *The C.S. Lewis Readers' Encyclopedia.*

Colin Duriez has published *Tolkien and C.S. Lewis: The Gift of Friendship, Tolkien and the Lord of the Rings: A Guide to Middle-Earth,* and *The C.S. Lewis Encyclopedia,* and is coauthor (with David Porter) of *The Inklings Handbook.*

Tom Shippey is a leading Tolkien scholar and the author of *The Road to Middle-Earth* and *J.R.R. Tolkien: Author of the Century.*

Jaume Alberto Poveda teaches at the University of Valladolid and has published articles in the *Journal of English Studies.*

K.S. Whetter is a professor in the department of English at Acadia University in Nova Scotia. His areas of specialization include medieval Arthurian tradition and Middle English romance, genre theory, and epic and heroic literature. His writing has appeared in such journals as *Reading Medieval Studies, Parergon, Year's Work in English Studies,* and *Mythlore.*

R. Andrew McDonald has published in *Mythlore* and appeared in the Tolkien fan film, *Born of Hope.*

Elizabeth A. Whittingham is the author of *The Evolution of Tolkien's Mythology: A Study of Middle Earth.*

Acknowledgments

Katharyn W. Crabbe, "The Quest as Fairy Tale: *The Hobbit*." From *J. R. R. Tolkien*, pp. 28–31. Copyright © 1988 Continuum.

Brian Rosebury, "*The Hobbit*." From T*olkien: A Critical Assessment*, pp. 100–05. Copyright © 1992 St. Martin's Press.

Humphrey Carpenter, "Enter Mr Baggins" From *J.R.R. Tolkien: A Biography*, pp. 179–86. Copyright © 2000 Houghton Mifflin.

Perry C. Bramlett, "*The Hobbit* and Other Works for Children." From *I Am in Fact a Hobbit: An Introduction to the Life and Work of J.R.R. Tolkien*, pp. 26–33. Copyright © 2003 Mercer University Press.

Colin Duriez, "Two Journeys There and Back Again: *The Pilgrim's Regress* and *The Hobbit* (1930–1937)." From *Tolkien and C.S. Lewis: The Gift of Friendship*, pp. 88–91. Copyright © 2003 Hidden Spring.

Tom Shippey, "The Bourgeois Burglar." From *The Road to Middle-Earth*, pp. 67–71. Copyright © 2003 Houghton Mifflin.

Jaume Albero Poveda, "Narrative Models in Tolkien's Stories of Middle-Earth." From *Journal of English Studies* 4 (2003–2004): 7–22. Copyright © 2004 *Journal of English Studies*.

K.S. Whetter and R. Andrew McDonald, "'In the Hilt is Fame': Resonances of Medieval Swords and Sword-lore in J.R.R. Tolkien's *The Hobbit* and *The Lord of the Rings*." From *Mythlore* 25, nos. 1/2 (Fall/Winter 2006): 7–9, 13–14. Copyright © 2006 by *Mythlore*.

Every effort has been made to contact the owners of copyrighted material and secure copyright permission. Articles appearing in this volume generally appear much as they did in their original publication with few or no editorial changes. In some cases, foreign language text has been removed from the original essay. Those interested in locating the original source will find the information cited above.

Index